BLOG, SCHMOG!

THE TRUTH ABOUT WHAT BLOGS CAN
(AND CAN'T) DO FOR YOUR BUSINESS

ROBERT W. BLY

NELSON BOOKS
A Division of Thomas Nelson Publishers
Since 1798

www.thomasnelson.com

Published by Thomas Nelson, Inc., P. O. Box 141000, Nashville, Tennessee 37214.

Nelson Books titles may be purchased in bulk for educational, business, fund-raising, or sales promotional use. For information, please e-mail SpecialMarkets@ThomasNelson.com.

Library of Congress Cataloging-in-Publication Data Available

ISBN-10: 0-7852-1576-X
ISBN-13: 978-0-7852-1576-9

Printed in the United States of America

06 07 08 09 QW 6 5 4 3 2 1

This book is for my nephew,
Daniel Sprecher

Are you spending too much time blogging . . . and not enough time getting productive work done?

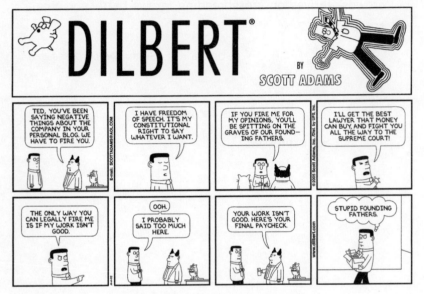

It is of the nature of ideas to be communicated: written, spoken, done. The idea is like grass. It craves light, likes crowds, thrives on crossbreeding, grows better for being stepped on.

—Ursula K. LeGuin, *The Dispossessed*

The cleverly expressed opposite of any generally accepted idea is worth a fortune to somebody.

—F. Scott Fitzgerald

Not everything that you think should be said. And not everything that you say should be written. And not everything that is written should be printed.

—Menachem Mendel (1787–1859)

I can't stand another minute of this mindless gab!

—*Dexter's Laboratory*, Cartoon Network

>> Warning <<

This is a highly idiosyncratic, personal, and opinionated book, written by a marketing advisor with a quarter century of experience, about blogging and in particular about the value (or lack thereof) of blogging as a marketing tool.

If you are a blogging evangelist or consultant, I guarantee you will hate this book and that it will make you angry.

If you are a practical marketer concerned with results, this book can prevent you from wasting a lot of time and money, improve your marketing results, and create *realistic* expectations about what blogging can—and cannot—do for your business.

As a side benefit, it may also save you a small fortune on consultant fees, not to mention a lot of wasted time, energy, and effort that would get you a better return on investment spent in other areas of your marketing.

CONTENTS

INTRODUCTION

WHAT'S ALL THE FUSS ABOUT BLOGGING?

Blogging, which in its most basic form is journaling online—but which also has ramifications much more far-reaching—gained national prominence in 2004.

BusinessWeek said that blogging was undergoing "explosive growth."[1] Merriam-Webster announced that "blogging" was the most frequently requested word in dictionary searches.[1a]

Eight million American adults say they have started blogs. One out of four Internet users reads blogs, and 12 percent of Internet users have posted comments on blogs.[2]

A number of bloggers are self-described "blogging evangelists." They believe blogging is an Internet revolution that will make conventional communication obsolete. Some derisively refer to books, magazines, and newspapers as antiquated "dead-tree" media, and they are convinced that blogging will become the most powerful form of marketing and media on the planet.

They may be right: according to an article published by the Illinois Information Technology Association (IITA), 550 million Internet searches are done daily worldwide . . . and only

23 percent of adults under age thirty read newspapers regularly anymore.[3]

Many bloggers express outright contempt for the mainstream media (New York City book publishers, national magazines, daily newspapers). They say the only way to get published in these dead-tree media is through either (a) luck or (b) inside connections.

Conventional publishing is certainly not in its prime: according to *The Week*, more than one out of three hardcover books are returned by bookstores to the publishers unsold each year. An article in *BtoB* reports that after 2006, Thomas Publishing will cease publishing the print edition of its industrial buying directory, *Thomas Register*, making it available online only.[4]

"Quicker than we probably think, print will be replaced by the online delivery system as the primary source of content," says consultant Malcolm Netburn in an interview with *Circulation Management*. "I look at my 15-year-old son and his friends, and I see where they get their information. And it's overwhelmingly, if not exclusively, over the Internet."[5]

If you are an author, a bibliophile, and a lover of the printed word—like me—this can't be happy news to you.

"What's going on, I believe, is a shortened national attention span," says Joseph Epstein. "People have lost patience, endurance, tolerance for the lengthy, possibly even the leisurely, presentation of culture, teaching, entertainment, and much else . . . everyone wants shorter takes."[6] In a world of short-take readers, blogs certainly fit the bill.

Rick Bruner, an active blogger and my polar opposite in all things marketing, questions the effectiveness of my use of traditional media—specifically, articles I write for *DM News*, the weekly newspaper of the direct marketing industry.

He, too, refers to trade journals and newsletters as "dead-tree media," and suggests that online communication, like blogging, is really where the most effective marketing is. I'm not so sure. So far my blogging has brought me a lot of fascinating discussions with bloggers, but hardly any posts from potential clients.

My *DM News* articles, on the other hand, bring me a steady stream of leads, all from the direct marketers who are my potential clients—because that's who reads *DM News*.

My dead-tree medium is highly targeted. I am not sure who reads blogs, but *DM News* has an audit-verified circulation of fifty thousand direct marketers, which is my target spot-on market.

Here's my quick take on online versus offline media: online is more high tech, more today's hot topic, more the flavor of the month, more appealing to the under-thirty crowd, and more interactive.

Online is easier to respond to, and the response and discussion is immediately visible to everyone on the Internet. The conversation can spread like wildfire, which is a real plus.

Offline is more traditional, more appealing to the over-fifty crowd, and has greater selectivity. Anyone can publish a blog, Web site, or e-zine (electronic magazine). That's why David St. Lawrence calls blogging "Citizen's Publishing."[7] But not everyone can get published in *Harvard Business Review* or the *Wall Street Journal*—or convince McGraw-Hill or John Wiley & Sons to publish their book.

And that's why these dead-tree media, unlike a blog, give

the author a certain status and credibility that self-published online writings, like e-books, do not.

The best tactic is a mixed-media approach. For instance, I am a regular contributor to dead-tree media including *Writer's Digest* and *DM News*. And I am the author of more than sixty books published by such mainstream publishing houses as Prentice Hall and Amacom.

But I also publish a blog, a free monthly e-zine, and downloadable free articles and special reports, all available on my Web site (www.bly.com).

Blogging enthusiasts see blogging as a meritocracy, giving a voice and open forum to anyone who wants to write and communicate. They find the notion of talented thinkers, experts, and writers getting paid for their content to be antiquated, and they chant the mantra that "content should be free."

Are they right? Is blogging a true communications revolution? Or is blogging an enormous waste of time and money, and the last publishing refuge of the inarticulate and illiterate? Or, as the comic strip *Doonesbury* puts it:

> Isn't blogging basically for angry, semi-employed losers who are too untalented or too lazy to get real jobs in journalism? I mean, if the market really valued what you have to say, wouldn't someone pay you for it?[8]

To find out, I launched my own blog in November 2004. Within a matter of days, several blogging evangelists reported that my blog came close to setting a record for number of "posts" when it opened. (A post is a comment a reader places on the blog in response to a blog entry made by the owner.)

In 2004, I became one of the most talked about people in the "blogosphere" (the online community of people who blog) when, in my column for *DM News*, I asked what I believe are some of the important questions about blogging: "Here's a question I've been curious about lately: should marketers add blogging to their arsenal of marketing tactics? Will it help sell more products and services? Or is it—as I suspect—an utter waste of time? A pure vanity publication that won't pay you back even one thin dime for your effort?"

What came next shocked me: a full-scale attack against me from the blogosphere. (You can see it by searching "Bob Bly blogging" online; search engines love blogs, and frequent blog posts are an amazingly effective way to optimize your Web site's search engine rankings.) I was called "an idiot," "a dinosaur," and "yesterday's expert"—all because I dared to question the bloggers' beloved, trendy new medium. Tad Clarke, former editor-in-chief of *DM News*, said my antiblogging article generated more reader mail than any other story he ran that year.[9]

It was apparent to me that the blogging evangelists and advisors themselves were not prepared to take an objective look at their own medium. What was needed was an *unbiased* report from an experienced marketer, an author with no financial interest in promoting blogging, who would reveal (a) the pros and cons of blogging; (b) the effect of blogging on marketing, writing, and the printed word; and (c) the effectiveness of blogging in its major applications, especially politics, technology, and marketing.

I provide that unbiased report in *Blog, Schmog!* and answer the following questions:

- Is blogging a new and important channel for publishing and communication? Or are blogs merely an outlet for frustrated writers to post their rejected ramblings online?
- Are blogs encouraging a broader audience to read and write? Or are they another vanity press publishing banal trash that "real" publishers would never even take a second glance at?
- In what ways have blogging and the Internet changed the face of writing, publishing, public relations, news, journalism, and the writing profession?
- Are blogs a powerful new tool for PR and branding online? Or is investing time and money in a business blog an utter waste?
- What is the role of blogging in online marketing? Its ability to drive traffic through search engines is proven beyond question, but will it ever match the effectiveness of online newsletters and e-mail marketing?
- Is the blogosphere—the interconnected network of blogs on the Internet—a revolutionary new force in global communications? And if so, is anyone in control?
- What is the Internet's effect on writing as a profession and on publishing as an industry? Will people still pay for content when they can get all they want for free online?
- What is the future of blogging? Will it be a dominant marketing channel in a decade? Or will it soon go the way of the dodo and the dinosaur?

After reading *Blog, Schmog!* you will be better able to (a) understand and participate in blogging, (b) create and write an effective blog, and (c) realize what blogging can and cannot do, and therefore not waste more resources than are prudent in your business-blogging activities. The book cuts through the enormous hype surrounding blogging, enabling you to get a true and accurate picture of blogging's potential as well as its limitations.

Blog, Schmog! combines three major components:

1. Observations and analysis on blogging—its importance, effectiveness, applications, and limitations
2. Commentary and conclusions on the effect of blogging, if any, on mainstream marketing and media, especially book publishing, periodicals, and online marketing
3. Practical, real-world tips—from me as well as the numerous blogging experts I correspond with—on how to write an effective, reader-oriented blog

The first two content areas ("content" is blogging and Internet terminology for writing and information) are explored in a narrative of *Blog, Schmog!* that forms the core of the book.

The third area, the practical blogging tips, are presented in sidebars. That way, someone looking solely for how-to advice can skip the main narrative and, by reading just the sidebars, quickly get the strategies and techniques of starting and running a blog.

In addition, a series of smaller boxed sidebars present the "Rules of Blogging," which are short, pithy observations on how the blogosphere operates. Taken together (they are collected in an appendix at the book's end), they provide the most up-to-date and objective picture of the blogosphere available.

Who can benefit from reading this book?

- *Bloggers*—Various sources estimate there are between five and eleven million blogs on the Internet today, read regularly by approximately 11 percent of Internet users.

- *Internet users*—Search engines give priority to blogs when rating Web sites, so if you do online searches, you will inevitably come across blogs—and you need to know how to read and interpret them, and determine whether the information they present is accurate.

- *Authors, writers, consultants, speakers, information technology experts, attorneys, owners of intellectual property*—One area where bloggers are getting a positive ROI (return on investment) on their blogs is self-employed professionals and small service businesses dealing with intellectual capital.

- *Internet marketers*—If your business model centers on a Web site capable of converting search engine traffic to prospects and paid customers, blogging is one of the most effective search engine optimization tools available.

- *Entrepreneurs*—Millions of small businesses are looking for ways to promote themselves online, and blogging is the least expensive: virtually free.

- *Marketers*—Ad agencies, PR firms, and corporate marketing departments are being asked at record rates to help their clients and companies start and run blogs as a means of getting closer to the customer, raising brand awareness, and stimulating sales.

- *Writers*—With some reports of writers earning from a few hundred dollars a month to as much as $100,000 a year to write blogs that promote products, services, and organizations, blogging may represent a new market for writing services.

■ *Corporate executives*—CEOs and other executives at major corporations, such as Sun Microsystems and Microsoft, are starting blogs and looking for advice on how to blog more effectively.

In this book, I won't address HTML, design, programming, or any of the technical aspects of setting up a blog except in cursory detail. Tools for creating your own blogs, and a directory of consultants who can help you use them, are listed in the appendices—and any Web site designer can set you up with your own blog within a day for a nominal fee.

This book is about the strategy of using blogs as a business-building and marketing tool, explaining how your time is best spent on strategy, not fooling around with programming or design.

This is in keeping with my belief that learning computer technology or the technical aspects of the Internet is largely a waste of time for marketers and entrepreneurs because it detracts from their core focus and productivity. It is not, as my colleague and Internet marketing expert Fred Gleeck would say, "the highest and best use of your time."[10]

For instance, I give PowerPoint presentations regularly but would never waste my time learning to use PowerPoint, since I can outsource the layout of my presentations to a freelancer whose fee is about one-tenth my hourly billable rate.

One other point: *Blog, Schmog!* is unique among business

blogging guides because most other blogging books are written by blogging consultants, enthusiasts, and evangelists.

These authors are not objective about blogging. Their livelihood depends on convincing you that you need a blog and should hire them to help you with it. They have a vested interest in persuading you to jump on the blogging bandwagon; I do not.

My book is written from the point of view of a blogging skeptic and doubter, not one who has bought into the whole blogging fad without holding it up to close scrutiny. And my conclusions about blogging, unlike those of these other authors, are not always favorable; my positions on blogging are highly controversial within the blogosphere.

I do have a favor to ask. If you have a comment, idea, technique, or success story related to business blogging, why not send it to me so I can share it with readers of the next edition of this book? You will receive full credit, of course.

Here's how you can reach me:

Bob Bly

Copywriter

22 E. Quackenbush Avenue

Dumont, NJ 07629

Phone: 201-385-1220

Fax: 201-385-1138

e-mail: rwbly@bly.com

Web site: www.bly.com

Blog: www.bly.com/blog/blog.htm

CHAPTER 1

Fear and Loathing
in the Blogosphere

Hell hath no fury like a blogger scorned.

It all began innocently enough.

In November 2004, I briefly became one of the most famous people in the blogosphere. The incident that started it all sent shock waves of fear and loathing reverberating throughout the blogosphere, the effects of which are still being felt and argued about today.

But first, thirty seconds' worth of introduction is in order.

My name is Bob Bly. I'm a freelance copywriter by vocation and a book author by avocation.

That means I make my living writing things like direct mail, white papers, brochures, catalogs, books, articles, and other print materials.

Well, it *used* to be print—or what Kurt Vonnegut calls "making idiosyncratic arrangements in horizontal lines, with ink on bleached and flattened wood pulp, of 26 phonetic symbols, ten numbers, and about eight punctuation marks."

But during the past few years, *online writing* has become a major part of my work: writing Web sites, landing pages, online ads, online newsletters, and e-mail marketing campaigns.

Of course, you don't care about me or what I do for a living personally. Nor should you.

But as you'll soon see, my writing and marketing background is extremely relevant to our discussion and analysis of blogs as a communications, political, social, PR, publishing, and marketing channel.

Anyway, one of the things I write is a regular column for *DM News*, the weekly trade paper of the direct-marketing industry. And that's where the trouble started.

As I mentioned in the introduction, in November 2004, I wrote a column in which I expressed skepticism that blogging was anything more than a passing fad or that it had any potential to be a significant weapon in the marketer's arsenal.

I wrote the column out of frustration and skepticism. I was reading a lot of loud, arrogant articles from bloggers proclaiming that traditional print marketing was dead, and that blogging would totally revolutionize marketing. And I just didn't see it.

Here's part of what appeared in my *DM News* article (the complete text is reprinted in appendix A):

> Most of the blogs I encounter are rambling, streams-of-consciousness musings about a particular topic of interest to the author, largely bereft of the kind of practical, pithy tips that e-zines, Web sites, and white papers offer.
>
> Reading the blog is like reading the author's journal or diary. And unless you are a guru or celebrity whom others worship from afar, people are simply not going to flock to your blog to discover your latest thoughts on life.

Another one of my complaints with blogs in particular and the Web in general is the ease with which people can post and disseminate content. "The best thing about the Web is that anyone can publish on it; the worst thing about the Web is that anyone can publish on it," a columnist for *Maximum PC* observes.

The problem is that there is already too much content, and we don't want or need more. Analysis, wisdom, insight, advice, strategies, ideas—yes. But raw information, data, or content—no. And from what I can see, blogs serve up almost none of the former, and tons of the latter.

Most blogs seem to be the private idiosyncratic musings of an individual, without censure or editing of any kind. And the result is like porridge: a gloppy mess, tasteless, and not very satisfying.

Until that changes, I can't see starting and maintaining a blog of your own, unless you are bored and looking for something to do, or require an outlet for self-expression. And if the latter is the case, well . . . why not just buy and keep a diary instead?

Now, I hate controversy. I live a peaceful, quiet life. My idea of the perfect day is to do absolutely nothing but sit at my PC for twelve or so hours (I am a recovering workaholic)—thinking, reading, and writing for my clients.

I should also confess that, before I started my own blog, I never read blogs. They failed to engage me, just as I never participated in online forums, chat, news groups, and other casual Internet activities, which seemed to me (with rare exception) a thundering waste of time.

When I wrote the *DM News* column, it was, to me, just another column. I had no idea what was about to happen, or that it would change my life over the course of the next year.

A few days later, my friend Deb Weil (www.wordbiz.com), a blogging expert and advocate, said to me, "How are you holding up?"

"From what?" I asked.

"From the rebellion in the blogosphere against you and your *DM News* piece!" she said. "You're the new antichrist of blogging. Haven't you even seen it?"

I admitted I hadn't. And as you'll see, that's part of the problem with blogging, and something the blogosphere doesn't seem to understand: there are millions of people who don't read, subscribe to, or ever see a blog.

Bloggers believe that blogs are all-encompassing, and that anything they say in their blog is somehow transmitted throughout the blogosphere and, by extension, throughout the entire world . . . even though the majority of people on the planet don't even have Internet access.

It's a cliché to say there are two kinds of people in the world, but in the case of blogging, it's true: those who read and post to blogs, and those who don't. The latter group, which accounts for the majority of people in the world today, will never see content posted on a blog.

RULE 1:
Not everyone blogs or
reads blogs, but bloggers sometimes
operate as if their blogs are
reaching everyone.

And of course, most people *aren't* reading blogs—yours or anyone else's. A study conducted in November 2004 found that thirty-five million Americans read blogs.[1] That means more than 80 percent of Americans never read blogs.

So I told Deb I hadn't seen anything about it. Of course I hadn't: I didn't (and still don't) subscribe to any blogs. "Go online," Deb advised me. "Search under 'Bob Bly blogging.'"

I did, and you should take a minute to do that now if you are near a PC. Go ahead. I'll wait. . . .

What I found was that she was right: overnight I had become this vilified, antiblogging thug, the arch nemesis of all that is good and holy about blogging.

Here are just a few of the comments, which range from bemused and pitying to kind and sympathetic, to seething anger:

David St. Lawrence:

It is a sad thing to see someone with obvious talent demonstrate to all and sundry that he does not understand what is happening in the world around him.

Bob Bly, a direct marketing guru of considerable repute, seems to have joined that distinguished roster of experts like Ken Olsen and Thomas Jefferson who could not grasp that technology had moved beyond their ability to understand it.

His article in *DM News* displays an amazing ignorance of blogging. It would appear that he relied on hearsay rather than direct inspection.

I am sure that he will get an earful of constructive criticism, now that he has revealed his impending dinosaurhood, but he may choose, like Dan Rather, to ignore the voices behind the curtain he has so carefully erected.

He is a nice guy, but does not understand that two-way communication trumps continuous outflow when it comes to developing relationships.

Rick Bruner:
Direct marketing copywriter Robert Bly argues that blogs are a big waste of time.

He doesn't know what he is talking about. One gets the sense he's only read about blogs in magazines. What else explains why he's still writing in that archaic dead-tree medium? Yeah, blogs are a waste of time with no provable ROI, but writing a one-time opinion piece in a magazine, whose Web page doesn't even link to Bly's crappy Web site, is ROI-riffic.

Oh, and how did I discover Bly's article in the first place? Through DMNews.com's e-mail newsletter? Ha! (Like I need to subscribe to another e-mail newsletter or trust my e-mail address to a company with "direct market-ing" in their name.) No, through a blog—duh.

Steve Hall:
Bob Bly, who's been a copywriter forever, doesn't like Web-logs. Expressing that opinion would be welcome if Bly had a proper understanding of that platform. After reading his article about the topic, it is clear he has no idea what he is talking about.

Apparently, Bly has only read the blogs of teenage girls. There are many fine, business-focused Weblogs with valu-

able and intelligent content for and by business professionals published today.

Blogs are only rambling incoherent diaries if they are
written that way. The Weblog publishing platform does not
perpetuate a particular writing style. It just makes it easier
to publish thought—good or bad.

And white papers? Who reads those anymore? All you
get out of white papers is high-level marketing blather and
who needs that? Oh wait, you do, Bob. Writing them pays
your salary.

Bob Cargill:

The great respect I have for Robert Bly is exceeded only by
how surprised I was to learn how little he thinks of blogs.
That said, I would be remiss if I did not call him out for his
unfounded—and, frankly unfair—criticism of blogs.

If most blogs he has encountered are "rambling stream-
of-consciousness musings," then he obviously hasn't seen
those smart, marketing-related blogs kept by the likes of
Tom Peters, Seth Godin, B. L. Ochman, and Yvonne DiVita,
to name just four.

Neville Hobson:

Here's a good example of someone involved in marketing
who either just doesn't get it or feels intimidated by a communication channel that he doesn't understand. There's a
bloke in the U.S. called Robert Bly who wrote an article
about blogs that simply illustrates a total lack of compre-
hension about blogging in a business context. It is indeed
the story of the copywriter who definitely didn't get it.

To dismiss blogs by saying they are a complete waste of time doesn't make any sense at all. As a communication medium, blogs today have clear credibility and increasing business influence.

Adriana Cronin-Lukas:
According to direct marketing copywriter Robert Bly, blogs are a big waste of time. Oh, good. I'm glad that's sorted out. Now I can go back to my boring job in the city instead of wasting time on this crazy blog stuff. Many (in the blogosphere) have descended on this clueless marketer. . . .

Marc Orchant:
It's all about the conversation. That's the point of the blog space. As a lifelong marketer, I find the DM industry to be behind the curve when it comes to embracing disruptive technologies.

My argument is that blogging is more likely to raise brand awareness. Therefore, I don't think it is appropriate to look for a close relationship between blogging and direct sales.

Yvonne DiVita:
First of all, you can't discredit blogging at this early stage . . . those e-zines and e-mail marketing campaigns did not return a positive ROI right out of the box. Come on! It took years.

E-zines and e-mail especially are two marketing tools that stand to get crushed by blogging—talk about too much content shoved into my e-mail box on a daily basis.

Blogging is going to blow them out of the water because RSS allows me to control what comes to me, what I want to have delivered, and when I read it. No spam, no filtering, no junk.

David N. Rosen:
You may have been too hasty in your recent dismissal of Weblogs for marketing purposes. Yes, there are plenty of solipsistic, rambling, personal diary types of blogs out there. But that's hardly the whole story.

What makes me think this subject is worth further consideration is the enormous success and influence of political blogs, which are having a huge impact on media and journalism. At this point, I think it makes sense to keep one's mind open on the subject of business blogging, and watch for new approaches and developments.

What shocked me—but won't shock you if you are an active participant in the blogosphere—is the vehemence and venom with which some of these people attacked me.

My friend Fred Gleeck says that every activity must be measured by its ROMD—return on marketing dollar. The bloggers I began to correspond with seemed to have no interest in determining whether ROMD could be established for blogging.

Instead, their minds were already made up: they were so enamored with the tool, the results seemed not to matter. "Blogging will revolutionize marketing," I was told time and time again. When I asked for one shred of evidence, most shrugged and called me shortsighted for daring to question the supremacy of the blog.

"Culture scanners have become next-big-thing junkies," writes Frank Salerno in *DM News*. "Any time a bright new thing bobs to the surface of the cultural bucket, they are eager to hold it aloft as a zeitgeist bender. This excessive eagerness can cause these enthusiasts to be hasty in their pronouncements."[2]

Here's what blogging really is and how it works

If you've never participated in, visited, or seen a blog, your first step in understanding blogging is to do so now.

Yes, I can and will explain blogging to you, but your understanding will be deeper if you *see* an actual blog rather than just *read* about it.

Appendix E gives the URLs of over thirty blogs that I find interesting or instructive, so you can start there. Or, you can visit my blog at www.bly.com/blog/blog.htm. Do it now before proceeding. I'll wait. . . .

Okay. Now that you've looked at some blogs, let's talk about exactly what you were looking at.

Merriam-Webster (MW), the dictionary publisher, defines a *blog* as "a Web site that contains an online personal journal with reflections, comments and often hyperlinks." MW reports that *blog* was one of the most looked-up words on its Internet sites this year.

"A blog is an online journal," explains blogging expert Deb Weil in her Business Blogging Starter Kit (www.wordbiz.com). "It's called a journal because every entry is time and date stamped and always presented in reverse chronological order."

The theory is that if you are a writer, an expert, or an information marketer—or, if you publish information to establish your expertise in a niche industry or field—blogging should be part of your publishing arsenal.

According to Deb, a business blog is "a platform from which to lobby, network, and influence sales. It's a way to circumvent traditional media and analysts. And blogging can be done instantly, in real time, at a fraction of the cost of using traditional channels."

Here, in a nutshell, is how blogs work:

- A blog is a specialized type of simple Web site.
- The main portion of the blog is an online journal in which the blogger (blog owner or operator) makes periodic entries called "posts."
- Only the blog owner can make, update, or edit entries in the blog.
- Anyone can visit the blog at its unique URL (Web address) and read it.
- Visitors can respond to the journal entries by posting their own comments, also often referred to as "posts" instead of "comments," which are appended to whatever entry the visitor chooses.
- Through hyperlinks, the blog operator can link his or her blog to other blogs or any other online content. These links can appear both within the posts themselves as well as in a list of URLs displayed on the blog.

The hyperlinks are a primary differentiator between blogs and traditional dead-tree media such as newspapers and books.

In magazine articles, writers sometimes include the URLs of relevant Web sites. But doing so is not central to offline writing, and readers often don't go to the sites, because in print, the links are static—you can't click on a URL printed in a magazine and go to the page referenced.

Hyperlinks are a critical part of the blogosphere. Links to articles and Web sites allow blog readers to drill down to greater levels of detail on topics being covered in summary fashion in the blog.

By putting links to other blogs, bloggers who share a common interest—marketing bloggers are a good example—can create a network in which they are all interconnected. Jennifer Rice (www.mantrabrand.com) says, "The beauty of blogging is that it's a medium based on digital networking."

Copywriter and blogger David Garfinkel says, "Blogging is a way of creating multiple inputs and outputs to your Web presence through inbound and outbound links, search engine listings, and references offline to the blog.

"The multiplexing potential is enormous. Blogdom is growing at an unbelievable rate right now. There are lots of things you can do with a blog that you can't do with any other medium: discussion forums on multiple topics, score 'points' with search engine spiders, get subscriptions through RSS, and leverage the potential of RSS subscriptions with frequent posts."[3]

John Jantsch talks about "blog channels," which he defines as "a group of very specific content blogs woven tightly together around a larger topic." Readers can subscribe to each blog or the entire channel via RSS.[4]

Another key characteristic of blogs is that, unlike a newspaper or magazine or even a subscription Web site, blogs are free. There is no charge to read or add comments to any blog, and literally anyone in the world with a PC and Internet access can do so.

Two immediate questions come to mind: First, why would anyone want to keep his or her journal online for all the world to see? And second, who on earth would want to read someone else's online journal?

As to the first question, reasons vary. Some bloggers are "content exhibitionists"—they have thoughts, feelings, ideas, or stories they feel compelled to share with the world, and blogs are perhaps the ideal forum for doing so.

"I blog to be part of a community of people I respect," says Phil Windley, a professor of computer science at Brigham Young University. "I want to understand their thinking, and I want them to understand mine. I blog to be part of the conversation. I blog to refine my thinking. I blog because I think I really don't understand something until I write about it."

Other bloggers ostensibly want to communicate with others, but their real motive is self-promotion: they want to establish themselves as gurus or experts in a particular field, industry, or profession, and blogging is one of the vehicles available for doing this.

Why people want to read blogs is less certain. As I've mentioned, search engines favor blogs, so people doing online searches for specific topics often find blogs among their results. But there are other people who deliberately seek out and prefer to read blogs as a medium, just as there are people who prefer Web sites, or magazines, or books.

On the surface, the affinity of some people for blogs is difficult for me to fathom: their content is not as well organized as most Web sites; not as complete as most books; and not as

clear or articulate as most magazine articles on the same topics. So what's the appeal?

I share the concerns and opinions on blogging expressed by
R. Myers in a letter to the editor of *BusinessWeek*: "I'm afraid
that citizen journalism will be 'junk journalism' filled with
opinions, rumors, lies, falsehood, and unreliable information.
Personally I don't want to spend hours at my computer sifting
through that stuff. Reputable publishers research reliable
sources, sift through and cull information, and present it in
well-written articles."[5]

Are most blogs self-indulgent drivel?

In the November 2005 issue of *Direct*, Ken Magill writes,
"Outside politics, 99.9 percent of blog entries are, well, horseblit linked to more horseblit."[6]

The reason, he cites, is that most blogs are written by people
who, in his opinion, don't write very well.

"The vast majority of people are not professional communicators for a reason," says Ken. "They don't do it very well."

He concludes that blogs are "the media phenomenon
responsible for the publication of more self-indulgent non-
sense than any other in the history of the world"—an opinion
I share.

Blogger Tony Dowler believes that Magill is way off base.
He says: "I disagree. This is a bit like walking into a coffee shop
and complaining that the conversations there don't live up to
the standards of a university classroom or a television news-
room.

"Never mind that you stand a good chance of finding at
least one conversation that's better. The bulk of blogs aren't

meant to be polished communications, and we shouldn't be concerned that they aren't.

"If this is a problem for anyone, I have a suggestion: learn how to find the good conversations. Find a high quality blog. See who they link to. See who links to them. You're on your way."

After spending more than a year reading a lot of blogs, I remain sided with Magill, not Dowler, on the question of blog quality. Yes, there are some good blogs. But the medium as a whole suffers from a lower standard of quality than other media it competes with.

Now, am I wrong, or has technology—specifically, the Internet, desktop publishing, and printing on demand—reduced two of my favorite things in the world, books and writing, to mere commodities?

When I started out as a writer at Westinghouse in the late 1970s, managers who wanted to demean the craft of writing called it "word-smithing."

But I think that the true demise of the craft was signaled when people began referring to writing as "content", which, like pork or butter, sounds like something you buy by the pound.

Certainly, with 150,000 books published every year, we're suffering from a new kind of pollution—"content pollution." There's simply too much to read and not enough time to read it.

I worry that every time I write in my blog or write an article or a book, I am contributing to this content pollution.

After all, aren't there already a million others already writing on the same topics and saying the same things? And isn't that true for virtually every author—and every topic—on the planet?

When I expressed this concern on my blog, marketing

expert Justin Hitt responded with a logical argument on why new writings are not "content pollution" even though a topic has been thoroughly explored by other writers:

> Yes, others are writing similar materials, even whole books on the exact topics presented on this and other blogs. I haven't read all your books, so it's even possible you're echoing those same materials here.
>
> But deep down inside everyone there is the desire to get that one little bit of new information, even if we have to wade through what we already know to find it.
>
> Smart marketers will utilize these facts to capture the attention (and curiosity) of prospective buyers—and even smarter writers will become information collectors and organizers for even busier end-users.

Still, with so many poorly written, wordy, sloppily conceived blogs cluttering the Internet, I could not, for the life of me, understand why people bothered to read blogs at all, much less subscribed to them for regular doses of blog writing. So I posted the following question on my blog:

> My question has to do with why you visit, read, and leave posts on blogs (like this one).
>
> There are so many other sources of information available on the topics you are interested in: Web sites, articles, books.
>
> Most of these sources are (in my opinion) better written, better researched, more authoritative, and more thought out than blogs. Do you agree?

So why not just read books, periodicals, and Web sites? Why do you read blogs . . . and bother writing posts on them?

The topic generated some heat, with forty or so replies. Answers from my blog readers showed me that there are, in fact, multiple reasons why bloggers prefer their blogs to other reading. . . .

Ten reasons why blogging enthusiasts read blogs religiously

From the forty or so replies to my query, "Why do you read blogs?" as well as a few other sources, I've compiled these ten advantages of the blogging medium that compel readers to return to their favorite blogs again and again, both to read what is written as well as post their own comments—an impulse I unfortunately never could feel to any significant degree during or after my own year in the blogosphere.

Note here and throughout the book that some sources are well identified, with name, title, and affiliation; others are just a first name or an e-mail address. I only have the identification each person posting to my blog chose to provide:

1. *Blogs are uncensored and unedited.* Blog readers have a preference for raw, unedited content, unfiltered and uncensored by the mainstream media. "It's nice to read material that is relatively unedited," writes Eric. "It gives you quicker insight into a person's thought processes or personality to read text that hasn't gone through the PR-speak . . . unsanitized reading material."

2. *Blogs give you a voice.* When you read something in the newspaper you don't agree with, you probably just set the

article aside. Once in a while, you might write a letter to the editor and hope that it gets published. But even then it would likely be cut down for space.

When you read something you don't like or agree with in a blog, on the other hand, you can talk back immediately, and have your rebuttal published on the World Wide Web—literally in seconds.

"It is a people-to-people communication," says Alexey V. "It is personal."

My colleague, consultant Joel Heffner, adds: "Today's friendly (and sometimes not so friendly) conversation has moved, at least for some, onto blogs. For many, I think, that's why they read blogs and add their own comments."

"I think self-expression plays a big role in why people blog," says my friend, copywriter Steve Slaunwhite. "If you removed the feature on your blog that allowed people to include their names with their posts, I suspect that participation would take a serious nosedive."

3. *Some say blogs have superior content quality.* It's my contention that books and articles are superior to blogs in both content quality and writing. But many blog enthusiasts disagree.

"For certain arcane topics, like search engine optimization, blogs offer more late-breaking news and insight than trade pubs that would normally cover that kind of thing," says Derek Scruggs. "I'd rather read the thoughts of someone who's an actual SEO expert, not the summary of those thoughts from a reporter for a marketing magazine."

4. *Blogs are personal.* The blog is the product of one individual working independently, not a team of reporters or a corporate committee. Writers express in their blogs whatever

thoughts come to them that moment and communicate those thoughts instantly to their blog subscribers.

"Most blogs are just more accessible than straight news reports," writes Donald Baker. "You get to know the blogger's interests and biases more surely than in a straight news publication, and a blog's informality makes it a lot easier to get information across.

5. *Blogs enable the reader to connect with the author directly.* Like a bulletin board or forum, blogs permit the creation of "threads." In a thread, a commentator writes an opinion or statement, which is permanently posted on the Web.

Visitors to the blog, board, or forum can read the statement and reply. Their responses, once posted, become permanently available on the blog, board, or forum for others to read and reply to.

The blog author, of course, sees it all. And the majority of blog authors I read pay close attention to posts on their blogs, often replying to those comments on the blog. So you can talk directly with the authors of the blogs you read, although the conversation will be public. However, many blogs have a link that allows you to e-mail the author, so if you have a private comment or query, you can make it, even though there is no guarantee the author will reply.

6. *Blogs provide intellectual stimulation.* Bloggers find the act of reading and posting on blogs to be intellectually engaging. Says Jim Logan: "I blog because it makes me think. I learn from what excites people, what gets them talking, and what leaves me speaking in the 'dark.' I've learned from comments left on my blog. Blogging makes me better at my profession."

7. *The blogosphere is a community.* The Internet lends itself

to the formation of "communities of interest," defined as groups of people with similar interests who congregate someplace on the Internet to share information, exchange ideas, and talk about their favorite subject. Examples include Web sites, chat rooms, forums, and, now, blogs. Jim Logan says, "I've met and joined conversations with people across continents."

"I've met some terrific folks that I would not have met otherwise," says blogger Yvonne DiVita. "It's more personal, albeit, in a virtual world." Indeed, the blogosphere is like a club, and anyone can join.

8. *The blog is a nonrestricted publishing outlet.* There are thousands, maybe millions, of people who have something to say but cannot find an outlet for their words in the traditional venues of book, magazine, and newspaper publishing. Starting a blog gives these people a ready outlet for unlimited self-expression at virtually no cost.

9. *Blogs offer a greater level of immediacy and interaction than print media.* If an industry is covered by a weekly trade magazine, you may not find out about a current big story until the next week's publication. But a blogger with a story can disseminate the news in seconds.

"When something is happening, I can read what other people are thinking and saying—people who I know, either through their writings, or just through their blog," says Zapsel. "Note that, unlike a book, or even a newspaper, there isn't an editor who is intervening."

10. *Blogs provide information not obtainable elsewhere.* "The blogs I read are mostly ones that provide information that I cannot easily obtain in print or elsewhere, such as topics on technology and travel," says Jeff Barry.

"I do read books and magazines," says Jim Logan, "but the blogosphere provides such a smorgasbord of information, cool tips, and personalities that it's a little like visiting Manhattan: there's so much energy and humanity, and it's all right here for me."

Doesn't everybody need an editor?

One of the things bloggers like best about blogging is the ability to instantaneously publish their thoughts on the Web without editing or censure of any kind.

But that begs the question: is every thought of everyone on the planet something that should be published?

You get the sense in the blogosphere that no one is in charge. Bloggers are not held to the same standards as paid, professional journalists.

When you write a letter to the editor of your local town newspaper, a professional, the editor, decides whether it will be published. He also edits your letter for style, brevity, and grammar. Rich H., who has edited a number of my books, recently noted in an e-mail to me, "Everybody needs an editor!"

Copywriters, magazine writers, newspaper reporters, and book authors published by traditional publishing houses all have editors. But self-published book authors, e-book authors, e-zine writers, and bloggers usually don't; what they write goes straight from their PC to the reader, without being vetted by a third party.

I've often heard blogging enthusiasts derisively refer to "edited content" when speaking of traditional publishing. But is editing bad? I've always thought of editing as "quality control" for the written word. And as a rule, give me good writing over bad any day.

What do you think? Do you prefer having your writing edited or left alone? Would you rather read blogs and other "unedited" writings or magazines where the text you are reading has passed through an editor's "quality inspection"?

Why I *don't* read blogs

When it comes to traditional forms of reading, writing, marketing, and public relations versus blogs, it is never, of course, an either/or situation; you can read (and write) books and articles as well as blogs. You can conduct an e-mail marketing campaign or publish an online newsletter and also publish a blog.

Having said that, I've noticed that there are bloggers for whom reading and writing blogs is their preferred medium: they actively seek out blogs to read and subscribe to those blogs through RSS feeds, which we'll discuss in chapter 2, that alert them when new content is posted on their favorite blogs.

As much as I tried while writing *Blog, Schmog!* I could never muster much enthusiasm for subscribing to or reading blogs, even the blogs of people I know well. Whether or not you like blogs mainly boils down to personal preference. Some people like to read short stories, while others prefer novels.

For me, the main turnoff of blogs is the tremendous amount of time it would take for me to subscribe to, visit, read, and post on blogs of interest to me. I find magazines, books, and Google searches much more time efficient.

When you subscribe to a blog through an RSS feed, you are

notified via e-mail every time the blog owner makes another post to the blog. Do you really want to get an e-mail from me every time I jot down a new thought?

If you post a comment in response to a blog entry, you are likely to return several times to see what reaction it has generated on the blog. In this way, blogging becomes terribly time-consuming and quite possibly addictive.

Writer Patrice Robertie comments:

> The problem with blogs, it seems to me, is that they presume the reader can and will make time to check them out regularly. But how many blogs can an individual hope to follow and still get their work done and have an offline life?
>
> Am I the only one out here who is actually starting to limit the time they spend online? I mean, it's so easy to think, "It will just be 5 minutes," and then you see almost an hour has gone by. And sometimes it's more fun to be doing this than doing my work!

In particular, a lot of the marketing and PR consultants who blog seem to me to spend an inordinate amount of time talking on each other's blogs about how great blogging is and how the rest of the world just doesn't "get" blogging. By that, they usually mean that anyone who doesn't agree that blogs are a marketing revolution, or that every company should have a blog (as many blogging consultants not surprisingly advocate), is clueless.

So I simply don't have the time to read blogs. Or, more accurately, the time I do have I choose to invest in other activities, including reading and writing books and articles.

But then, I was never a fan of online forums and chat rooms either, two media that have a lot of the same feel and characteristics of blogs.

When I first got online eons ago, I opened an account with CompuServe. I was fascinated to discover all the online forums where people with similar interests could congregate, chat, and share ideas and information.

My fascination lasted for not much longer than a day, because I found the conversation banal: most people seemed to have endless time for mindless chatter. After that first day, I rarely visited online forums, except for occasional research on behalf of a copywriting client.

In an issue of *BMA Marketing Notes*, marketing consultant Eric Gagnon makes the following comments about blogs:

> I [am] an avid Weblog reader. I spend my early morning reading my list of a dozen or so Weblogs and news sites instead of the morning paper. In fact, my wife says I spend too much time reading Weblogs. (I think she spends too much time on eBay, so it's a standoff.)
>
> But reading news, culture, and media pieces written by interesting, articulate people who seem to have lots of time on their hands is an entirely different form than the typical subject matter generated by most B2B companies, because the "good stuff" a company has to say is usually so valuable that it should remain under wraps.
>
> It's a fact that most of the really interesting and readable stuff that someone would want to see in your company's Weblog is stuff your company would be better off keeping to itself, like the inside scoop on a new joint ven-

ture, a new direction in business development, or a new product idea or observation.

This information comprises a company's core knowledge base and, as such, is far too valuable to be blabbed on a blog. Everything else either isn't very interesting, or is more effective if it's disseminated to, and published by, your industry's trade media.

The exception to this would be B2B companies in the "information business": Consultants, publishers, analysts, etc., who make a living by disseminating information and opinions. Here, blogging is another form of information distribution and communication, great self-promotion, and an interesting way to spread new ideas around in an industry.

Otherwise, don't be fooled by the hype surrounding Weblogs and other "Web 2.0" developments coming down the pike. The same thing goes for RSS feeds, podcasts, tags, video blogs, etc.

A daily podcast for Amalgamated Tool and Die Company? Get real! Most people in B2B environments (that is, outside the small coterie of Webheads who are pushing this stuff) are too busy to use these new features. Maybe one day, but not now.[7]

The vicious, irrational attack of the bloggers

When I wrote my *DM News* article in November 2004, I had no intention of getting involved in blogging.

My position was this: I love what I do, and what I do is (a) write direct-marketing copy and (b) write nonfiction books, articles, and columns—most (but not all) about business, marketing, writing, and related topics.

Over the past few years, I've become very involved with marketing online, which I don't view as terribly different than direct marketing offline . . . although, as you'll see, that's a viewpoint that puts me at odds with the blogosphere, too.

My main impetus to write my skeptical blogging article was that Deb Weil—a friend active in blogging—was actively preaching the virtue of blogging to the marketing community, and well, I just didn't buy it.

My logic was as follows: as a direct marketer, I'm only interested in marketing that generates a significant, measurable, and immediate return on marketing dollars, or ROMD.

Direct marketing, whether online or offline, does that. When you send out a direct mail package or a postcard or an e-mail marketing blast, you can measure the responses, leads, orders, and revenues it generates down to the penny.

Direct marketing thrives on sales, revenues, results, response—hard numbers. In direct marketing, you can't hide. If my direct-mail package pulls a 1 percent response and yours pulls a 2 percent response, than yours is better than mine, flat out, and subjective judgment does not enter the picture.

It's for this reason that so many copywriters, ad agencies, and marketing consultants stay away from direct marketing. They don't understand it or know how to use it, and the easy ability to measure sales results would quickly reveal that they are at best incompetent, at worst frauds.

Unable to make the cash register ring, these consultants and agencies still have to earn a living. So what do they sell? The nebulous, fuzzy concept of "branding"—a concept which *BusinessWeek* says is rapidly losing popularity with the big Fortune 500 advertisers.

In branding, advertising creates an awareness of a product gradually, over an extended period of time, often—but not always—at great expense in both time and money.

But two factors are conspiring to turn branding, once the beautiful swan of marketing, into its ugly duckling: economic pressure and the efficiency and measurability of online marketing.

Through economic pressure, a weakened U.S. economy and increased global competition are causing big corporations to tighten their belts and demand a visible, measurable, rapid ROI from every investment, from operations to marketing. Direct marketing can usually give it to them, but blogging and other brand-building activities often can't.

Blogging is one of the few forms of online marketing in which sales cannot be directly traced to a specific message or marketing effort, the results tabulated, and the ROI calculated. E-mail marketing, landing pages, online ads, and e-zines, by comparison, can all produce a quick and tangible ROI.

It is dangerous to make generalizations about a group, and it borders on prejudice. But it is necessary if we are to understand blogging and bloggers.

As a rule of thumb, bloggers tend to favor things that are new and trendy, rather than tested and proven, probably because bloggers, in my experience, tend to be young.

According to a doctoral thesis on blogging written by James Milne, 92 percent of bloggers are under the age of thirty: 51 percent are teenagers, while 40 percent are in their twenties. Personal blogging is a young person's medium, while business bloggers are typically in their twenties, thirties, and forties. An article in *BuzzMachine* reports that blog readers are more likely to be broadband users, be college educated, and have higher incomes.[8]

The older business bloggers, from their pictures and writing posted on their blog, are often men over sixty with a ponytail or big, bushy beard, hoping the free speech and trendiness of blogging might give them that old 1960s feeling of being revolutionary, countercultural, cool, and hip.

And overall, 56 percent of bloggers are female.

The attitude of blogging enthusiasts toward me and my skeptical view of blogging span the gamut of responses and emotions.

The largest group of bloggers to respond to my article felt that anyone in marketing who didn't love and embrace blogging was a "fuddy duddy," stuck in the old modes of communication (like making money, perhaps?) and unable to comprehend the new modes of communication (like spending all one's time chatting on the Internet for the purpose of making "conversations" that are the supposed real goal of marketing?). Their emotions on the issue ran from pity to contempt.

A few were kinder, taking it upon themselves to educate me so that I might be rehabilitated from my hard-sell ways and join in on their conversation.

A minority of bloggers were outraged, feeling they had the right to say anything they wanted about and to me, in any language that suited them.

"You're a moron," said an anonymous critic without the courage to identify herself or himself in an e-mail to me. (I noticed that a lot of militant proponents of the triumph of the Internet over print like to hide behind the anonymity the Net provides when speaking out on this issue or taking others to task.) "Your reasoning is flawed to the core. The worth of a blog is measured by the merits of a blog alone. If you want censure, editing, and 24-hour news cycle, read a newspaper."

And that's one of the bizarre comments many bloggers make: blogging is better than mainstream media (like newspapers and books) because it is not edited. To me, that's like saying you don't want to buy a car because the manufacturer has a quality control department.

In *Psychology of Weblogs*, John M. Grohol, Psy.D., observes:

Online communities have been around since the 1980s; (newsgroups are a good example). Blogs do little to inherently forward community, since the vast majority are a one-to-many relationship. There are, of course, exceptions to this rule, popular group blogs such as MetaFilter and Slashdot being two such examples.

There are bloggers and commentators who have written about how some blogs make the Web interesting again, because of their witty commentary or ability to find obscure, interesting links on a particular subject. The fact is, though, that there has always been interesting commentary online. Instead of it taking the form of a brief opinion spurred on by the discovery of a "new" link (new to them, anyway) or news story, it was instead in the form of essays found on Web sites offering a more in-depth look at a particular subject or current event.

Does brief commentary versus 1,200 word essays offer something inherently more interesting or unique? Well, unique, yes, and quite fitting for the attention deficit disorder nature of the Internet.

But a new, shorter essay or commentary format is not fun to read if the writer isn't consistent or doesn't say something interesting (again, in a consistently engaging manner). And that's the problem with blogs, and with the Web in general.

Most people are not great writers, and their ability to engage the reader is seriously lacking in most people's personal blogs. Lack of consistency is another big problem, in both writing style and quality, as well as in quantity (e.g., regular updates on a regular basis). Blogs simply don't work when the author isn't committed to maintaining them regularly in a qualitative way.[9]

There's a vocal group of bloggers—perhaps a minority, but a vocal one, to be sure—who think writing should not be edited, anyone in the world should be able to publish anything at any time, and the greatest virtues writing can have are (a) immediacy and (b)accessability—that is opinions can be expressed by anyone without regard to clarity of thought, quality of writing, or credentials of the author.

Some bloggers have a propensity to use jargon to make simple concepts sound more complex than they actually are. David St. Lawrence, a militant blogging evangelist, wrote to me: "Communication, in the sense that I use it, is not outflow nor is it inflow. It is the process of originating an idea that is received and enabling the recipient to reply and be duplicated on the sending end. In this way understanding occurs. Blogs, when done well, are conversations." There's that dreadful word *conversations* again.

Bloggers pretend to listen, but many are really deaf

It wasn't scary to get blasted by these bloggers for the simple reason that these folks are not my clients.

My client base is serious direct marketers—as well as medium and large corporations who are not direct marketers but sometimes use direct marketing to promote their products and services. Business bloggers, on the other hand, are ad agencies or consultants specializing in non-direct-response online marketing or branding—not my client base at all.

But I did find it frustrating that the bloggers attacking me seemed (a) unwilling to even consider the possibility that their medium might not be the new future of communication and (b) indignant and even angry that someone would even dare to suggest the idea.

So I began—selectively, of course—to respond to some of the criticisms, explaining as simply and clearly as I could where I was certain their logic was wrong, while challenging them to provide measurable evidence of the superiority of their approach.

My challenge was simple. One of my biggest clients was, at the time, generating annual online sales of approximately $40 million through such traditional online marketing methods as e-mail (which most of the bloggers who wrote me disdain) and online ads (today their annual online sales are more than $100 million).

I sent a challenge throughout the blogosphere, asking one blogger to step forward and show me a company that was generating just $400,000—1 percent of what my client was making—through their blog. Not one blogger who criticized me could produce such evidence.

Although my readers in the past have occasionally praised my clear and persuasive style of explaining marketing ideas, I did not achieve such an effect with the bloggers, who only became more incensed that I dared to challenge the power of the sacred blog.

What amazed me was that some bloggers are so fiercely loyal and vested in the success of their largely unproven medium that they refuse to even consider logical, factual proof that blogs may be a less-than-ideal channel for persuasion and communication.

For instance, blogger B. L. Ochman accused me of setting up some sort of elaborate PR scam with my antiblogging article: "Bob Bly is looking for a way to build readership for his column. He wants to get bloggers talking about him to build links to his column."

As a print guy, I don't even think of my articles as having "links," because I only see them as ink on paper, which I read when my issue of the magazine arrives in my mailbox. I certainly don't do anything to build readership to my column other than write the best, most interesting, most useful column I can.

I replied to Ms. Ochman and other bloggers: "You can see from my column that I don't consider blogs influential or important . . . so why would I want the blogosphere to talk about me? I think what you and others in the blogosphere miss is that there is this huge portion of the world that isn't 'into' your stuff. We don't read blogs, make posts, or visit chat rooms."

That observation helped me formulate Rule 2 of the blogosphere: bloggers have an unshakable prejudice that any communication that takes place online is automatically better than almost any communication that takes place offline. Based on that logic, senile Aunt Betty's blog about a Martian Santa Claus stealing her cookies at Christmas has just as much validity as a front-page story about Enron in the *Wall Street Journal*. And if you believe that, I have a bridge I want to sell you.

RULE 2:
Many bloggers believe that the Internet is better than print, period.

Ms. Ochman then concluded that, even though I am a columnist for a national marketing trade paper, not being a blogger disqualifies me from commenting on them: "You see, Bob, I don't follow sports, so I don't comment on them. In fact, I keep my posts and the many articles I write to topics I know a lot about. When you start reading blogs, and get yourself up to speed on the latest research and articles about them, your opinion about blogs will start to matter."

In other words: I won't listen to you unless you're on my team and agree with everything I believe! Also, I can take one spoonful from a bowl of chili and know whether it's good or not, even though I can't cook.

I give in to pressure and launch my blog to record-shattering results

After my antiblogging article in *DM News* was published, I received dozens of e-mails and posts like B. L. Ochman's telling me in essence that (a) I didn't understand blogs at all and (b) since I was not an active blogger, I had no right to comment on blogging in my article.

I found this to be a bizarre attitude, and, of course, I disagree with the premise that only a blogger can judge blogs. This would be like saying that only a fry cook can say whether a cheese omelet is good or bad, or only an automotive engineer can complain when the used car the dealer sells him turns out to be a lemon.

While not exactly famous, I have been involved as a practitioner in marketing—mostly as a freelance copywriter—and have been writing about it in books, trade articles, and columns for more than twenty-five years.

Readers of my column in *DM News*, which goes to fifty thousand subscribers weekly, read the publication, and my columns, for guidance, commentary, and advice on marketing topics—and business blogs are a marketing topic. I also publish a monthly online newsletter on marketing, *The Direct Response Letter* (see www.bly.com), which has more than forty thousand subscribers.

Therefore, as a columnist for the major trade publication in direct marketing, I think I have every right—as much as or more than anyone else—to comment on whether blogging is an effective marketing method.

Yet the comments nagged at me. It was true that I was not a blog reader. I had given a cursory glance at a few blogs and, frankly, found them to be banal and boring. And B. L. was right: I did not have a blog of my own.

Since blogging did not seem likely to go away anytime soon, I figured I was likely to write about blogging again, especially if the blogging boom continued rather than faded.

And to do that with the most authority, and therefore give the most value to my readers, I decided two things: I would start blogging—both reading blogs as well as posting comments on them. And I would start my own blog.

Starting a blog, as the blogging evangelists had told me, was indeed relatively straightforward and easy; and to help you start your own, chapter 2 shows you all the steps you have to take, and all the resources you need. I had my blog up and operating within two weeks of having published my antiblogging column and the ensuing online dust-up.

In my blog, my very first "post" (entry in the online Weblog), which I titled "How Direct Marketers Think," dealt with what I perceive as the difference between the practical, pragmatic, results-oriented mind-set of direct marketers and the soft, feel-good, warm-fuzzy, "build a brand" mentality of the blogosphere and their ilk(see page 37).

One of my first blog readers, Anita Campbell, responded with this thoughtful and sensible post on metrics for measuring a blog's effectiveness:

> Many people assume that the comments on a blog reveal the popularity and readership. I would suggest that is one measure for some blogs, but it doesn't apply at all to other blogs.
>
> It's all a question of the blog's purpose and style. Some blogs have a lot of community, with regular loyal readers. Other blogs get a ton of inbound links, and not just from other blogs, but from influential business sites and very popular e-zines.
>
> I've noticed an interesting dichotomy. Some of the sites with the most comments have surprisingly small numbers of inbound links, and vice versa.

It really boils down to who is perceived as a thought leader or opinion leader. And that is a complex question that can't be answered from looking at the face of a blog. You have to look at server traffic logs, inbound links (and not just links from blogs), subscribers to the blogs' e-zines and RSS feeds, e-mails, media requests, comments—the whole mix.

Oh, and you have to look at ROI—does it lead to compensation? And there's no way that a third-party observer can measure a blogger's ROI from a casual outside-in view.

Increasingly, companies are setting tangible, quantifiable goals for their blogging efforts and measuring the metrics, which is what blogging needs to become anything more than a trendy fad.

Example: eHobbies.com says it has watched its conversion rate double from the normal 2 to 4 percent whenever site users visit one of its blogs. Since adding blogging to its site, 5 percent of the company's overall traffic comes from its main blog destination, www.ehobbies.blogs.com. In addition, 5 percent of all orders have recently tracked to a blog-based coupon.

"I've scored a monthly marketing column in a national magazine and four clients from my blog," says Kirsten Osolind, a branding consultant. "Indeed it has helped me monetize the value of my company's services and products. More importantly, our blog helps us search optimize our business."

HOW DIRECT MARKETERS THINK

In this blog, I want to provide the blogosphere with a view from my side of the fence as a member of another "sphere"—

old-fashioned direct marketers who still believe the main purpose of marketing is to get the cash register ringing and not just have "conversations."

To start off, let me share with you what I believe is the "mind-set" of direct marketing, based on my quarter century in the business:

1. Direct marketers are only concerned with one thing—ROI (return on investment). That is, if you spend a dollar on a mailing, do you get two or three dollars back in sales?

2. Direct marketers don't care if other marketing experts or the general public finds their promotions loud, unappealing, too hard to sell, or behind the times. We only care if those promotions work.

3. Direct marketers know that often ugly and crude outperforms beautiful and sophisticated. Not always, but often.

4. Direct marketers know that subjective opinion about copy and creativity counts for squat. The only way to determine whether my copy is better or worse than your copy is in an A/B split test—not subjective judgment.

5. Non-direct marketers get very excited about new media and methods early, despite the fact that they have not proven their ability to generate positive ROI—and largely, it seems to me, because they are new. They are very eager to spend time and money on new vehicles that have not proven themselves in the marketplace.

6. Direct marketers, on the other hand, are cautious and

conservative. We want to know something works before we spend money on it. And even then, we conduct small tests to make sure it will work for us before rolling out with it on a larger scale.

7. Non-direct marketers are obsessed with branding, awareness, and image. Direct marketers consider ROI the primary objective, and we resist having our promotions being controlled by any branding requirements that might interfere with achieving it.

8. Direct marketers are increasingly finding that what works offline—direct mail, space ads—works online. Yes, there are some differences. But strong-selling copy is needed to secure the order, whether from a DM package or a landing page.

9. Direct marketers expect to see immediate ROI from their marketing efforts. Non-direct marketers hope to see their efforts change behavior or attitude in the market over a much longer horizon.

10. Non-direct marketers take extra pride in campaigns that are creative, clever, edgy, funny, or splashy. Direct marketers couldn't care less about such things, and some of us even look down our noses at them.

I led with this list as my first post for two reasons: First, I wanted to establish the tone, content, and premise for my blog, which I envisioned as a forum for education and open discussion on the particular mind-sets, methods, and approaches direct marketers take to generating sales that bloggers and branding folks seem to either ignore or disdain.

Second, based on the reaction to my column, I knew this was a topic that generates some heat and passion among business bloggers, who are overwhelmingly branding advocates and not direct marketers, and therefore would serve to stimulate posts in reaction to my list—both on my blog and other blogs.

Bloggers consider blogging an ideal medium for "having conversations" online, and they think of this as an essential thing. Marketing bloggers endlessly quote from and refer to *The Cluetrain Manifesto* (Perseus Books, 2001), which has as one of its major mantras: "marketing is conversation." Direct marketers, of course, know that marketing is not so much about having conversations as about making a sale, and we'll dismantle the silly *Cluetrain* notion of conversation later in the book.

Anyway, picking as my first entry a powerfully stated discussion of the differences between direct marketers (my camp) and non-direct marketers (the blogosphere) worked extremely well in both starting a conversation on the topic as well as helping my new blog make a splash and attract a lot of attention.

A number of the marketing blogs that roundly criticized me as a behind-the-times dinosaur after publication of my antiblogging column now ran feature stories on their blogs announcing the start of my blog and congratulating me for getting with the program, although some accurately noted that, far from jumping on the "blogging bandwagon," I was merely conducting my own test of the medium. In the remaining chapters of this book, I will report what I learned from that test, representing a full year of active participation in the blogosphere.

HOW OFTEN SHOULD YOU WRITE IN YOUR OWN BLOG?

One thing that was unclear to me at the start was how often to write a journal entry in one's blog.

From an ROI point of view, one should make the fewest entries necessary (because of the time required) to generate the most posts, traffic, and buzz.

Blogging advocates see the ability of blogs to create buzz as one of its strongest attributes. As a report from the Center for Media Research notes, buzz "can embolden or embarrass its subjects. It can affect sales, donations, and campaign coffers. It can move issues up or down, and reframe institutional agendas."

From a pure "fun" point of view, one should make a new entry whenever one has something interesting to say.

However, it's probably best to wait and make that fresh entry when the amount and frequency of posts made in reaction to the current entry diminishes to a negligible volume. If you post earlier, you rob yourself and your readers of ongoing, active conversation on a topic they are still interested in and that has not died down.

Yes, they can still post to that old entry, but in my admittedly limited experience in the blogosphere, I've noticed that most of the focus and action seem to revolve around the freshest entry.

My friend, and blogging authority, Deb Weil, says: "If you've launched a blog and are not posting new entries once a week or so, you're not blogging enough. The name of the game is fresh. Fresh content, fresh ideas, fresh ways of thinking, fresh links."

Derek Scrubb offered me this pragmatic, time-thrifty advice: "For you, blogging should be thirty minutes a week, tops." He suggests I simply post my *DM News* articles on my blog with a comments link. That seemed to me boring and unnecessary; the articles are readily available on the *DM News* Web site as well as the articles page of www.bly.com.

"The frequency of posting generally relates to the length of the posts," says David St. Lawrence. "If you are writing essays with thought-provoking content, one every few days may be just right.

"I think the best advice is to write from the heart as often as you feel you have something important to say. That way, visitors will always find something of value. When a blogger writes to a schedule, i.e., anything to fill space, the blog soon feels dead, like recycled ad copy."

IT professional and blogger Robert Kostin says that on his blog, Robertopia, he follows these posting guidelines: (a) no more than once a day (unless he has a short second posting), (b) no less than once every two days (except for holidays), and (c) no more than two hundred words per post.

"I post whenever I have something I want to convey," says copywriter Susanna Hutcheson. "But I do think one should post at least one or two entries each week at a minimum—depending on how long the post."

"I think the answer to how often and how much depends on what you expect from your blog," says Lloyd Lemons. "I do know this: recently I had large gaps between my posts, for various reasons, and my visitor totals fell off dramatically."

B. L. Ochman has had a similar experience. "Whenever I stop blogging for any period of time, traffic falls off, but it comes right back when I post," she says. "And the more controversial I am, the more traffic I get." My own experience shows both observations to be true.

"My advice is to write the blog for fun, and when you have a specific goal besides generating dialog, like highlighting a column or article, or promoting a report or seminar, include that too," says Susan Heywood.

"I notice that if I wait too long between posts, I see the effect on our mail order sales. My experience is similar to B. L.'s in that traffic returns when I post after a dry spell."

Amy Gahran comments, "Contrary to popular wisdom, you don't have to post blog items every single day. It's more important to post quality content. Few people read a given blog every day."

Jim Krukal says: "I think the worst mistake you can make is blogging just because you haven't in a few days. If you don't have anything to say that is helpful or fresh, then why say anything? Forcing a blog entry doesn't work; your readers can tell. Overall, if the content is good, no matter how much you post, you'll keep an audience."

Whatever you do, keep your blog active. About a year after I started my own blog, I got so busy that I didn't post to it for a month. Readers thought it had been abandoned, and readership of the blog dropped off dramatically.

Prior to that, my posts typically generated ten to forty comments or more each. After I started my blog up again after a four-week absence, each new post generated only a couple of comments. Conclusion: to keep readership high, you have to post frequently.

RULE 3:
**Add a new post to your blog once
or twice a week. Never go more than ten days
without adding a new post.**

CHAPTER 2

How to Start Your Own Blog

Frequently I am asked by companies and individuals, "Should I start a blog to promote my business?" My answer is: it depends.

There are certain types of businesses that can benefit from a blog, if not by driving direct sales, then at least through buzz and PR. These include:

- *Businesses that deal with intellectual capital.* Consultants, software engineers, designers, and other businesses that sell ideas gain a marketing advantage by establishing the validity of their methodology, style, approach, or philosophy. A blog is an ideal forum for creating that advantage, and for building your reputation as a recognized expert in your field. It also gives visitors to your Web site what they value most: good content.
- *Businesses that deal with topics their customers like to read about or talk about.* There are product categories that customers are emotionally or intellectually engaged with, and these make good topics for blogs. Examples include personal computers, digital photography, coffee, running, and travel. A blog is less likely to be effective for

a product category that customers are not passionate about or even interested in, such as dry cleaning or cat litter. *Cats*, however, would be a good topic for a blog.

- *Businesses whose customers are information seekers.* If you sell saltwater aquariums, that hobby requires a huge amount of knowledge on the part of the hobbyist, and a blog would be a great forum to share knowledge and experience. Saltwater aquarium hobbyists love to discuss their fascinating hobby, and the hobby requires a lot of information to be successful. On the other hand, if you sell goldfish and goldfish bowls, those pets require minimal care and no expertise to maintain, and owning a goldfish is a casual experience—more of a home decoration than a pet or hobby.

- *Businesses dealing with topics that are controversial or frequently updated.* If there is a lot of controversy or disagreement on your topic, blogs can provide a great outlet for customers to express their views. Example: the changing role of IT and key issues affecting the IT profession, such as outsourcing programming and help desks to India. If a topic changes frequently, a blog can be where you keep your customers up to date. Example: complying with regulations like ISO 9000, OSHA, or the Health Insurance Portability and Accountability Act's (HIPAA).

- *Self-employed professionals.* If you offer a service, it is to your advantage to establish yourself as a recognized authority or "guru" in your field, whether it's management consulting or quality assurance. Writing a blog is part of an overall strategy for becoming a recognized expert in your field, along with such other activities as writing articles for trade publications and giving speeches.

- *Technology and businesses.* IT and other technical people are early adapters of blogs and enjoy actively discussing the latest technology on them. A blog by a programmer or scientist can be an effective way to keep customers and other interested parties informed and enthusiastic about your company's technology. Blogs about industries, business topics (e.g., leadership), and specific companies can also garner substantial readership.

In his book *Blogging*, Biz Stone writes:

Small to medium-sized companies will benefit from having a company blog—a blog operated by one person or a small team passionate about its work. The kind of blog I'm talking about is different than the organized "Community Leader" approach taken by Macromedia.

A company blog doesn't necessarily exist to answer questions or respond to bug alerts. A company blog may do some marketing or bragging, and it may post relevant updates, but it can also be humorous or even off-topic at times.

The idea is to get people coming back, to gain their trust and offer them something worth reading. At the same time, the company blog provides information about products or services. Once a following or readership has been established and people have built up trust, they feel they "know" the president of the company. And that's good PR without really trying to be. It's authentic.[1]

Now, assuming you fall into one of the above categories and writing a blog would be beneficial from a marketing point of view, the questions become: "Do I want to do it?", "Do I have the resources to do it?" and then "What's my ROI?"

There is disagreement between blogging consultants and me about the time and effort required to maintain a blog. Those who unreservedly recommend a blog for every business and professional on the planet argue that blogging is not time-intensive and takes only an hour or two a week.

But in today's busy world, having to devote an hour or two a week to maintaining a blog is a commitment you might not want to make. And while a blog can be fun and exciting to start, the work of having to do it daily, especially if you, like me, are not a natural-born blogging enthusiast, can quickly become tiresome.

Worse, once you start a blog, you have to keep posting to it at least once or twice a week. Even a few weeks' absence can cause readers to believe you have abandoned your blog, decimating the readership you worked so hard to build.

The blog may take only an hour or two a week to write. But if you are a blogger, it consumes a greater share of your mind: you are constantly thinking about your topic as it relates to your blog, whether things you do and read belong on your blog, and how to keep your blog lively and active. It can become more consuming than you might wish, eating further and further into your limited reserve of time and mental energy.

If you are a self-employed professional, you most likely have to write your blog yourself, and that can stretch your already-filled schedule even thinner. If you are a marketing professional at a company, someone at your company is going to have to take responsibility for the blog. That could be you, an outside writer you hire, or, more likely, either a subject-matter expert or a high-level executive.

The advantage of having a blog written by a subject-matter expert is that information-hungry consumers get valuable tips and advice firsthand from a genuine authority on the topic, without having it filtered through, and watered down by, multiple layers of corporate approval and the marketing department.

The advantage of having a blog written by the CEO is that customers get firsthand intelligence on the direction and mission of the company from its leader. Also, when the CEO writes the blog, no one else has to approve it, so there is no delay between composition and online posting.

Quality writing: not for blogs?

Another question that comes up is: do you have to be a good writer to write a blog?

I am tempted to say that the quality of writing and thought appearing on blogs is inferior to other media, such as newspapers and magazines. And although that in fact is my impression, I would be hard-pressed to prove the point through precise quantitative measurement.

Look around and you can find intelligent, well written blogs on the Internet on virtually any topic. And you can also find amateurish, inaccurate, sloppy blogs on those same topics.

Do the crappy blogs outweigh the great ones? Of course. It may be true that 90 percent of blogs stink. But recall Sturgeon's law, proposed by science-fiction writer Theodore Sturgeon. He said, "90 percent of everything is crap." Blogs are probably not much different in that regard than books, magazines, newsletters, and TV shows, although perhaps the ratio of crap to quality is a bit higher in the blogging world.

This begs the question: does quality matter that much? There are two camps among readers when it comes to blogs regarding the concern over quality of communication. And neither one is right or wrong; which one you join is a matter of opinion and personal preference.

The first camp, of which I am a member, doesn't enjoy or read blogs, precisely because they are, for the most part, amateur efforts. Am I a literary or old media snob in this regard? Obviously yes.

The idea of blogging presupposes that (a) everyone can write and (b) everyone has something worth saying. Unfortunately, just the opposite is true: most people can't write well, and while almost everyone has original thoughts, ideas, and feelings, most of those should not be published.

But in today's online, video age, does bad writing really matter on blogs or anywhere else? "Standards of English grammar, usage, and style have declined perilously," says author Don Hauptman. "And yes, it matters. Literacy, civilized discourse, communications, and clarity are affected by the way we use language."[2]

Have you ever stumbled upon a diary and, even though you weren't supposed to, begun reading it? It's fascinating for the first two pages and then coma inducing after that. I feel much the same way about 99 percent of the blogs I see.

With the Jayson Blair scandal at the *New York Times*, we have learned that even that venerable newspaper does not always print news that's fit to print. And the Oprah flap with

James Frey's memoir *A Million Little Pieces* turning out to be fabricated in many parts revealed a shocking fact about traditional book publishing: that most publishers don't fact check the books they produce; they rely on authors to do that.

The fact remains, however, that traditional media does a lot more fact checking and editing than blog writers, who do virtually none. Therefore their quality and accuracy are largely superior. As an example, I recently wrote a short article for a large consumer newsletter. For virtually every fact I quoted, the editor demanded either a source or more detail. Bloggers are not held to the same rigorous standards for reporting and writing that journalists and even authors must meet.

The other camp of bloggers is made up of readers who clearly prefer blogs over other media. Why do they have this leaning toward blogging? Many tell me they love blogs precisely because they *are* unfiltered and unedited. "A white paper is 'promotional pap' from a marketing department—pure PR BS," a blogging consultant told me. "A blog is the raw truth, going directly from the writer's keyboard to the reader's screen."

There are clearly people who are attracted to and seek out blogs. I have found no statistics to support this, but I have noticed that on many blogs, the majority of posts are made over time by a small core group of readers who seem to spend an inordinate amount of time checking the blog and commenting on it. My suspicion is that the wide market out there is much less influenced by blogs than the blogging consultants are trying to sell to their clients. In reality, a small, albeit vocal, minority of your customers and prospects read blogs and respond to them.

The quality of the *content* on many blogs is also questionable. Some blog readers praise blogs for allowing the reader to have a conversation directly with a subject matter expert (SME) without interference from an editorial "middle man."

But magazines and other traditional media have an advantage most blogs don't: a staff and budget for original research and reporting. On many blogs I encounter, the blogger is not creating original content, but commenting and giving an opinion on something he or she read elsewhere.

In traditional media, at least some attempt is made to ensure that commentators, editorial writers, and reviewers have some qualification or credential to talk about the subject, or at least that their comment is well thought out and fair.

In the blogosphere, however, anybody can say anything about anything. And therein lies the problem.

In Robert B. Parker's Spenser novel, *Cold Service*, private investigator Spenser says this to his girlfriend Susan about his sidekick Hawk: "He's nearly always right. Not because he knows everything. But because he never talks about things he doesn't know."

This is a good tip for bloggers, writers, speakers, and anyone else who communicates: stick to what you know and you'll be a more effective, more persuasive, more credible communicator.

And by "knowing" a thing, I don't mean just researching and reading about it. I mean knowing from actual experience.

The only way to ensure total credibility as a blogger is not to blog on a subject unless you've actually done it. If you haven't done it and a reader challenges you, you are completely vulnerable because you don't totally know what you are talking about. And the last thing the world needs is one more uninformed opinion, right?

RULE 4:
A blog is not going to reach all your customers. The only way to ensure you reach every customer is through direct marketing, e.g., sending an e-mail, postcard, or letter to your house file (customer mailing list).

Measuring blogging ROI

Lord Kelvin, inventor of the Kelvin temperature scale—the only temperature measure that does not require negative numbers to measure absolute zero, the temperature at which all molecular movement ceases—said, "When you can express something in numbers, then you know something about it."

By that measure, branding gurus and general ad agencies know very little indeed about producing measurable marketing results.

As reported in *BtoB* magazine, a new "Marketing Accountability" study found that 73 percent of senior-level marketers reported a "lack of confidence in understanding the sales impact of a marketing campaign."

If they had interviewed direct marketers, I think the number reporting confidence in understanding the sales impact of their marketing would have been much higher.

The lesson: if you want to increase ROI from your marketing and be able to measure and prove that you did so, shift your efforts away from branding and general advertising and toward direct marketing.

Here's where I believe most blogging consultants today

deserve to be scolded. Many have proclaimed that blogging is either a communications revolution or the most powerful marketing tool created this century. These blogging consultants convince clients that (a) blogs are an essential component of their marketing strategy and (b) blogs will deliver incredible marketing value. But here's the problem: they can't prove they are right, yet they act as if they can.

An article in the January 10, 2005, issue of *BusinessWeek* predicts that going forward in marketing, "The focus will be on return on investment (ROI)." But it is, in many cases, difficult to prove a positive ROI from blogging, because blogging is an image, awareness, or PR tool, and not a direct-response medium.

With e-mail marketing, you can precisely measure the ROI of every e-mail marketing message you send as long as you have a specific offer and give the recipient a means to respond to it in a way you can measure. For instance, you can measure click-through rates for e-mail marketing—the number of people who click on the hyperlink in the e-mail to get more information. You can also measure the number of people who, after reading the Web page they click to, fill in their information on that page to request a white paper download, software demo, Webcast, or whatever the offer is.

With a blog, you can get a qualitative sense that people are reading and talking about your blog. Many bloggers report higher search engine rankings for their Web site after starting a blog. Mindjet, a software company, tested blogs for driving Web site traffic and found them equally or more targeted and cost effective when compared to ads with Yahoo! or Google.

But unlike direct-response marketing, in which every inquiry and order can be traced to a specific promotion and the sales generated by any promotion can be calculated to the penny, blogging's benefits are more nebulous, less tangible, and more difficult to measure.[3]

That's not necessarily a bad thing, and it doesn't mean blogging can't be very beneficial to your business. But it does mean that to call blogging a "marketing revolution" or proclaim blogging to be the most potent communications tool in your marcom arsenal is overstating the case, or at least making a claim you can't back up with hard facts.

If your business meets any of the criteria for companies that can benefit from a blog listed earlier in this chapter, and you have the time, skill, and desire to write a blog, by all means add a blog to your online marketing communications mix. But treat it as what it is: an adjunct to a total marketing communications program and not the cornerstone or foundation of such a program.

Have realistic expectations for blogging, and by that I mean modest expectations, and you won't be disappointed. Expect blogging to live up to its hype and revolutionize your business, and it is unlikely to live up to your expectations.

RULE 5:
Blogging, like public relations and image advertising, may have a substantial effect on your business, but the precise ROI is extremely difficult to measure.

SIX QUESTIONS TO ASK
WHEN STARTING YOUR BLOG

1. *What is your goal for the blog?* Do you want to disseminate updated information on your product? Get users
   talking about their issues so you can design product
   upgrades to better meet their needs? Overcome mis-
   conceptions about your product in the marketplace?

2. *Who is your target audience?* Anyone can go online and
   read your blog, but for marketing purposes, a quality
   audience is more important than quantity. And even
   though people from all walks of life are going to see
   your blog, don't write it for them. Write it for your target audience, in their language, with the content at
   their level. For a marketing blog, the only readers who
   matter are customers and prospects.

3. *How are you going to measure success?* Are you going to
   measure unique visits to your Web site generated by
   organic search before and after you begin your blog?
   That's one of the few metrics you can measure somewhat accurately in a quantitative sense.

   At least one blogging consultant I know of measures
   her success by how many awards her blog wins, which
   is ridiculous. She also measures it by how much publicity her blog generates in the mainstream press, which is
   valuable and sensible.

4. *Who's going to blog?* Is it the head programmer? The
   product designer? The plant manager? The marketing

VP? The CEO? Think about who your audience would want to hear from and why. Tip: the person who is the subject-matter expert on the topic of the blog is probably the best candidate to write it, whether independently or with help from a blogging consultant, writer, or editor.

5. *How are you going to manage the ongoing feedback loop that the blogosphere provides?* Imagine you are the marketing director of ABC Company. You log onto your Web site and find someone has posted a comment on the blog saying your company is a bunch of crooks and your products suck. Are you going to leave that up? Delete it? Respond to it?

   Or, say you are reading an independent blog and find the writer bashing your technology. Do you respond to it or ignore it?

6. *How will you integrate your blog with your regular Web site?* Will the blog be its own Web site with an independent URL? Or will your blog be a menu button choice off the home page of your main Web site, as I have done at www.bly.com?

Source: Elisa Camahort, *Worker Bees*

RSS feeds

In a recent survey, copywriter Nick Usborne asked readers of *Excess Voice*, his newsletter about writing online, whether they prefer RSS feeds or e-zines.

The results:

- 49 percent had no idea what an RSS feed is.
- 31 percent said they are RSS fans and prefer it to e-zines.
- 20 percent said they subscribe to some RSS feeds but don't see them replacing e-zines.

According to the Pew Internet & American Life Project, only 5 percent of Internet users say they use RSS aggregates or XML readers to get news and other information delivered from blogs and content-rich Web sites.

"E-zines give you an intangible benefit simply because they appear in someone's in-box at a particular moment," comments Usborne. "With RSS, you run the risk of losing that sense of immediacy, of being in the reader's mind in the here and now."

What is RSS? To begin with, it's one of those things everyone says is easy to understand. And it is, as soon as you have your own "ah-ha" moment.

RSS feeds enable you to sign up for content, from both blogs and e-zines, so you get it as soon as it's made available by the author. That way, instead of having to check your favorite blog to see what's new, you get an e-mail notifying you every time the blog author adds a new post to his or her site.

The easiest way to explain it is to walk you through an example of RSS in action. I'm not going to try to explain everything on the subject (largely because a lot of it is above my head), but this should help get you started.[4]

Let's sign you up to an excellent e-newsletter on online copy-writing, *Excess Voice*, published by my colleague Nick Usborne.

If you want to read the *Excess Voice* newsletter every two weeks, you can either read it in your e-mail in-box or read it in your Web browser.

You already know how it works when you subscribe to a newsletter via e-mail. You sign up, hope the spam filters don't block some or all issues, and then read the newsletter in your e-mail program, whatever that might be.

With RSS, instead of subscribing via e-mail, you subscribe via a Web page.

If you have a Yahoo! account, go to My Yahoo! and click through to the Add Content page. On the right side of the Find Content area, you will see a link that reads, "Add RSS by URL."

Follow that link and, to add the *Excess Voice* RSS feed, simply paste this URL into the field provided: http://www.excess voice.com/excessfeed.xml. Now click the Add button and you're done.

If you don't use Yahoo! register at Bloglines.com and follow the same process. Bloglines is a free service and is where you can read all the RSS feeds to which you have subscribed, and of course, it's geared toward blogs.

Now, whenever you go to Yahoo! or Bloglines, you will see when the *Excess Voice* feed has been updated. In Yahoo! it will tell you how many hours or days ago the feed was updated. In Bloglines the feed name will appear in bold, and a number after the name will tell you how many items within the feed have been updated since you last checked. When you check the *Excess Voice* feeds, you will see that with each feed, you don't get the complete content. You will see only the title and the first ten lines or so of content—just enough so you can decide if you are interested or not.

If you want to read the whole article, for example, click on the link provided and you will be taken to the page on the *Excess Voice* site where you can see the complete item.

Meanwhile, here is what the author is doing behind the scenes to deliver this information: he added one new document to the root folder of his Web site on the server— an XML file, "excessfeed.xml."

Within this XML file, he includes the necessary coding and the preview text and links you see in My Yahoo! or Bloglines. Whenever he adds a new article, review, or newsletter to his site, he updates the content in this XML file and uploads it to his server.

Yahoo! and Bloglines will periodically check that XML file to see if it has been updated. If it has, they will let you know in the ways described above.

The blog or newsletter writer can decide how many feeds he wants to create and how many items to have within each feed. You can even add small images. And you can schedule when the feeds are updated. For instance, with an e-newsletter, you can send out the newsletter broadcast at the same time you upload the revised XML file, so it is published by e-mail and on the Web at the same time.

What's an XML file? Don't worry about it. You can use a WYSIWYG software tool called FeedForAll. It provides a simple interface that enables you to create, format, edit, and upload your feeds.

Once you get the idea and have chosen your preferred RSS Reader (Yahoo!, Bloglines, etc.), you can subscribe to dozens of different feeds: news, newsletters, articles, blogs, and more. Sign up with one click and unsubscribe with one click (no more newsletter unsubscribe hassles).

More and more people are turning to RSS. They use it instead of subscribing to newsletters. They also use it to choose which elements of content they want to hear about from various sites.

If you have a Web site, you can have RSS content delivered directly to your site. You want the latest art and culture news from the BBC showing on your site, automatically updated? No problem. Hence the "Syndication" in RSS—Really Simple Syndication.

You no longer have to actively visit a long list of Web sites (or blogs) for information on specific topics or industry verticals. It comes to you automatically via the RSS feeds you've chosen.

Publishers can be sure that their blog or news updates are being successfully "pushed" to interested subscribers without being siphoned off into e-mail junk folders.

Some advertisers are looking to RSS as a new way to push their messages to targeted audiences. It remains to be seen whether blog publishers will accept this. Many blogging purists are already saying no to advertising within the editorial environment of a blog.

Bottom line: we're still in the early adopter phase when it comes to syndicating content via RSS. But it's slowly catching on, just as blogs are becoming more and more accepted as an online communications tool.

The Pew report found that only one out of every twenty Internet users gets content delivered through RSS. In my view, that won't increase substantially until the software is improved to make RSS much simpler to use. A study from JupiterResearch concludes: "Most marketers remain skeptical of using RSS as a mechanism to supplement their e-mail marketing newsletter content."[5]

"It will probably take another one or two years to see how things progress," says marketing consultant Joel Heffner. "If Internet Explorer incorporates RSS, millions of people would have easy access to RSS. The next version of Apple's browser will do that, as will Firefox and other browsers. When 'everyone' knows about RSS, then blogs will be that much more valuable."[6]

Picking a name for your blog

I don't think the name you give your blog is the key factor in its popularity or success, but a relevant name can certainly attract both quantity and quality of readership. Let's briefly review the limited number of choices available when naming your blog. There are four basic categories of names to choose from:

1. *Your name.* If you are a consultant or expert promoting yourself and you have built brand equity in your name from other activities (e.g., writing a book, writing a column, giving speeches), why not capitalize on that name recognition by using it in your blog? Blogger Max Bloomberg named his blog simply Max Bloomberg's Blog.

2. *Your company name.* For a larger organization, the brand equity or recognition is in the corporate name, not an individual's name. The Trade Show Marketing Institute (TSMI) calls their blog TSMI's Trade Show Report.

3. *Your topic.* Blogger Deb Weil is a consultant and pub-

lisher specializing in online communication. Since her business revolves around words, she named her business and blog WordBiz.

4. *A symbolic or representative name.* The blog Lip Sticking focuses on marketing to women online. General Motors has a car blog called the Fastlane Blog. Blogger David St. Lawrence has a blog called Ripples, which I get the impression refers to how blogging spreads thoughts out over the Internet, like ripples in a pond into which you toss a small stone. Paul Woodhouse's blog about sheet metal is called The Tinbasher.

You can also use a tool like www.wordtracker.com to determine which key words related to your topic are searched most often, and then incorporate one or two of those key words into your blog title.

Blog layout and design: choose your template with care

There are a number of popular tools you can use to set up your blog quickly and easily. These include WordPress, TypePad, Blogger, and a few others listed in appendix F.

It's already pretty inexpensive to set up primitive Web sites if you shop around and don't make your site too elaborate. But by doing your blog layout yourself with these tools, your cost can be zero, other than the expense of registering the domain name and hosting the site.

Of course, if you have programming or design skills, or hire someone who does, you can dress up your blog beyond the standard layouts offered by the blogging tools. You can find affordable Web site designers either at www.elance.com or on the Vendors page of www.bly.com under Web Site Design.

Blog sites like www.blogger.com and www.typepad.com

provide easy-to-use templates that help you get your blog published online as quickly as possible. Once published, you can easily customize your blog so that it projects an image consistent with your other marketing communications.

The easiest and most noticeable way you can customize your blog is by adding your photograph. A photograph adds personality that "voices" your message and sets it apart from your competition.

If you are setting up a business blog, the colors you use should match the colors used in your firm's other online and offline marketing. The key is to choose a palette—or selection—of colors that work well together.

Use colors to separate individual posts from other blog elements, such as headers, which contain the title of your blog and a brief description, and sidebars, with text and links that always appear next to posts.

You can also use color to unify the different parts of your blog. For example, set headlines for individual posts in the same color used in your blog's header. If you are publishing a team blog, you can format each author's posts in a different text color or type style.

You can easily customize sidebar options. Sidebars can be placed on the left, right, or both sides of your posts. You can customize background information, a philosophy statement, and e-mail links.

A category index can allow readers to review and retrieve old blog entries by categories you define. Your blog can also store archives of previous posts organized by date.

Banners for advertising and revenue links to URLs for e-books or teleseminar registration, or Google AdSense links, can be added to the blog in the margins. Calendars can display the days each month when you posted new content.

You can choose a default typeface, type size, alignment, and colors for headlines and text. You can also emphasize key words and phrases by using style variations such as bold, italic, and bold-italics. When appropriate, you can improve the looks of your posts by using bulleted and numbered lists.

When first starting out, many bloggers set their blog title and description in the header as text, formatted by the template. Later, however, you can replace the default header text with a header graphic created using the typefaces that match your corporate graphic standards. You can also add your firm's logo as a graphic in the sidebar.

If you publish a newsletter and want to encourage sign-ups, add a picture of it and a sign-up form to the sidebar.

In order to immediately publish your blog, you can create a URL for your blog based on your name and/or blog title in combination with your business's blog. These default URLs can be long, cumbersome, and hard to communicate. Examples: http://rogerparker.typepad.com/upcomingevents/ and http://rogerparker.typepad.com/newsletter_marketing/.

Once your blog is up and running, however, you create a shorter alias URL that redirects visitors to the original URL. For example, the following shortcuts redirect visitors to the original long URL: www.rcpevents.info and www.rcpnewsletters.info.

By the time you've finished modifying the blogging tool's standard template, your blog can reflect your firm's unique identity, style, and look. Although you may have begun with a "packaged solution," your blog will soon reflect an accurate and unique image of your firm or association.

That being said, the design or look of your blog is secondary to its contents. An attractive design may make a blog easier to read and more pleasurable to look at. Design may also reinforce the branding and image you want to convey. But nobody visits blogs to admire the graphics. People visit blogs to read your content and participate in a conversation about it. So don't spend too much time agonizing over blog design or pay thousands of dollars to a top Web designer to dress up your blog. It's not worth the effort and expense.

How to write a first entry that generates a record number of posts—and why you should want to do so

F. Scott Fitzgerald once said, "The cleverly expressed opposite of any generally accepted idea is worth a fortune to somebody."

A time-tested strategy that works in marketing in general and especially in public relations is to be controversial or contentious. People love arguments, and if you pick a fight with an established guru, authority, belief, or position, you can virtually be assured of getting wide readership and media coverage.

If you don't believe that people love to argue in print, write a letter to the editor of your local newspaper expressing your strongly stated opinion on a public issue such as the school budget or a new traffic light for Main Street. I can virtually guarantee the next issue will have at least three to four letters, half of which vehemently agree with your position and half of which just as vehemently dispute it.

As an aside, you can gain a lesson on how not to write by reading these letters. I believe the worst published writing in America is in letters to the editor of local town papers, with blogs a close second. A good editing exercise to strengthen your writing skills is to write a letter to the editor of your town paper and then revise and edit until you can get across the same message in the fewest words possible. You'll find that most letters to the editor can be profitably cut in half or less with no sacrifice in content, and the same can be said for many blogs.

Blogs in particular, because of their interactive nature, are the perfect medium for argument. The comment mechanism on blogs exists for people to respond to the ideas expressed on the blog, and as a rule, the comments are of two types: either they agree with the post or disagree with it.

On my blog, my first long post, reprinted in chapter 1, took a position I knew bloggers would find objectionable: stating that direct marketing is a more potent and powerful online marketing tool than blogs.

Within a few days, more than sixty people commented in response to my blog, and many of them began to pick up the thread on their own blogs. Suddenly I was all over the Internet, and everyone in the blogging and marketing communities seemed to know about me and my blog.

Don't pick a fight for the sake of being contentious, but if you are passionate about an argument, expressing your side of the argument on your blog is nearly certain to launch your blog with a bang, generating a high level of interest, readership, and response.

People love to argue, and blogs give them an open, public forum to conduct protracted and vigorous arguments on the Internet. If you stimulate and start such arguments by posting strong or contrary opinions on important issues related to your subject on your blog, you will likely generate a higher volume of readership and participation than a straightforward news, how-to, or informational blog.

RULE 6:
Blogs are, by nature, contentious. Arguments, opinions, and strongly held points of view all play well to the blog audience.

Encore: what to cover in your next five entries, and why this is so critical

When I saw the different discussions of the practical and pragmatic mind-set of direct marketers versus the idealistic and innovative mind-set of bloggers—and people responding to that difference—I continued discussing it on my blog.

As I blogged along, I noticed that some topics—for instance, my rants against branding as a waste of money, and my argument that marketing dollars should be shifted away from image and brand advertising to measurable, accountable direct marketing—generated a lot of heat, passion, and an increased number of comments.

Quickly, I identified the handful of topics that created this kind of excitement and enthusiasm, and deliberately reasoned that, based on the large number of comments each post generated, these were the topics that engaged my blog readers most. And so I concentrated on those topics. On my blog, they included:

- The Internet, writing, literacy, and publishing
- Paid vs. free content online
- The ineffectiveness of branding and the superiority of direct marketing

Sure enough, when I wrote a post on one of these topics of interest, I would get ten to twenty-five posts. When I strayed to other topics, the number of posts would drop to half a dozen or so.

Of course, not every post should be contentious; that would quickly wear thin. But if you see subscriptions and participation flagging, you can stimulate interest in your blog by picking a friendly fight or argument.

This should arise naturally from your own beliefs and opinions. Blogs are not neutral and were never intended to be so. They are meant to reflect the viewpoint of the blog author, and the more strongly they do so, the more interesting they are.

One of the big advantages of blogs over most other forms of communication is the immediate and in-depth reader feedback. Comments give you an instant reading of how well you are doing and whether your message is resonating with your audience. A blogger whose goal is not mere self-expression but rather communication and influence will to a degree cater to the interests of his readers, like any good publication editor will do.

More ways to increase blog readership and participation

Blogs are more fun and exciting when there is a lively discussion going on. My own blog generated more than sixty posts within twenty-four hours of my putting it up online, which Paul Chaney, a marketing consultant and blogging advocate, says is an unusually high volume.

Is that because the blogging community wanted to see what I (a self-confessed blogging skeptic) was up to? Or because my first entry naturally stimulated conversation?

Maybe. But I bet part of the reason was that I ended with an invitation to respond.

In direct marketing—online or offline—we call this "asking for the order."

Whenever you post something interesting or controversial, close your post by explicitly asking for the reader's position. One of my favorite closing lines for posts to my blog is simply to ask the reader, "What do you think?" Other examples are: "Am I accurate here? Or way off base?" "Is this on the mark, or do you handle it differently?" "What say you?"

I know bloggers are aware that they can respond to blog entries with their own posts, but as a direct marketer, I know that when you ask for a response, you get more responses.

Another technique that stimulates discussion is, rather than say my opinion is fact, admit in my posts that I am not sure of my position and want the readers' feedback.

Particularly when your post takes an unpopular or controversial stance on a hotly debated issue in your industry, if you are hard-nosed about your position, the quality of comments may reflect mainly anger or vehement disagreement. But if your post is more in the nature of seeking other opinions, you are more likely to get constructive, helpful feedback and appreciation from readers of your open-mindedness.

Here's something else I do that's unusual. When people leave a link to their site on the signature to their post, I sometimes (not always) click on the link and e-mail them a personal thank-you for their post.

I also occasionally answer, by e-mail or even phone, questions that they asked in their post but are too complex or situation-specific to adequately address in my blog.

Perhaps this is taking the idea of conversation to a ridiculous extreme, and it is certainly not time efficient, but my instinct says to do it. Most have responded positively. A few tell me that, to follow good blogging etiquette, all comments should be posted on the blog, not sent in private communication.

I'm not so sure. What do you think?

Other blog-writing tips[7]

1. *Start with a topic you're passionate about.* This is your theme, the thread that will run through your blog. You had better be passionate about it, because you'll be chipping away at it for months. Yes, that's the bad news. It takes time to build your blog into something worth reading. It's the accumulation of posts (or entries) over a period of months or longer that will set you apart as a real blogger.

Let's say you start a blog to promote your own career. Ideally, your topic should be related to your job hunt. If you're searching for a position in sales, for example, you might develop a blog that focuses on "the close." All the different ways to get there; what works and what doesn't; examples or case studies based on your current experience, etc.

2. *Concentrate on shorter, more frequent entries in your blog.* Now for the good news. You don't have to write a long essay each time you post to your blog. On the contrary, a short paragraph or two is plenty—sometimes a sentence will suffice. Your goal is to show that you're knowledgeable about your topic, that you're reading other related blogs or news sources (on- or offline).

In fact, a sentence or two with a link directing readers to a relevant article in the *Wall Street Journal* or other respected periodical is plenty. The fact that you noticed the article and have an opinion about it is what counts.

3. *Let yourself go as a writer; let your authentic "voice" emerge.* Good blogs have a viewpoint and a voice. They reveal something about the way the blogger thinks—as well as what he or she thinks about. This is where it gets a bit tricky, however. You want to be honest and forthright in your writing.

But you don't want to cross the line by saying things that are critical or inappropriate about your current employer or major players in your industry. The best advice is to use common sense. Every time you post a new entry, remember that you are creating a public Web page, easily searchable by Google.

4. *Use correct grammar and syntax (no misspellings allowed, just as on your resume or your site).* This leads me to another tip: if you're blogging your way to a new job, the quality of your writing really does matter. As a refugee from the corporate workplace myself, I can tell you that the ability to write is in woefully short supply at most companies.

No matter what type of position—or new client—you are pursuing, a blog is a way to demonstrate that you can write and think clearly, concisely, and concretely. That will put you head and shoulders above most candidates. Oh, and yes, you must use proper grammar and spelling no matter how informal the tone of your writing.

5. *Purposefully organize the content of your blog.* A blog provides you with an elegant and easy-to-use writing tool. It is also a mini content-management system. Use it purposefully. Think about the categories you want to cover over time. Are there keywords you should be using that recruiters or potential employers may be searching on?

Create a category for that phrase. In addition, title each of your posts with care. Include as many specifics and keywords as possible. If you're quoting an expert or brand-name company in your blog entry, include the name in your title. Your blog entry may show up in search engine results alongside the Web site for a Fortune 500 company.

6. *Post a new entry at least once or twice a week.* Circling back to tip number two, you need to write frequently in order to keep your blog fresh. The more you post, the more content you are creating. Since each new post or entry is its own Web page, you are increasing the chances that search engines will find your blog.

One way to force yourself to write more often is to use your blog as a place to park an interesting tidbit of info or useful URL. When you run across something you'd like to write about, open up your blog and create a draft entry. Give it a provisional title. You can come back later when you have twenty minutes to spare and can write a coherent paragraph.

7. *Include your key contact information on your blog.* You'd be amazed at how many bloggers forget to do this. Never forget that your blog may turn up in a recruiter's or potential employer's Google search. By building your contact information into your blog template, you make it easy for him or her to pick up the phone and call or send an e-mail.

Additionally, it's proper etiquette to indicate where you currently work. It is also perfectly acceptable to add a phrase such as "The views expressed are my own."

8. *Have fun when you blog.* Whether you're blogging your way to a new job or new customers, you may find that blogging is truly a creative outlet. Over time you might find your-

self teasing clarity out of a complex topic or delving into subjects you didn't know you were so interested in. Keep chipping away with each blog entry. Who knows? Your blog might turn into a book, as it has for so many of your fellow bloggers, including me!

CHAPTER 3

BLOGETIQUETTE:
THE RULES OF BLOGGING

- -

Have you noticed that the standards of polite conversation and civil discourse established offline are not adhered to online?

That applies to blogging as well as to other forms of online communication, such as e-mail.

For instance, I publish a free e-newsletter. It is an opt-in newsletter, which means you can't get it unless you sign up for it. We don't send it to people unless they request it at www.bly.com, and therefore, it isn't spam.

But once in a while, someone gets it who either hasn't subscribed, thinks he hasn't, or maybe doesn't remember signing up—and he thinks it is spam.

At times, the reaction of these people to getting a harmless e-mail they believe is spam borders on how you and I reacted to, say, 9/11: outrage of an almost inconceivable scale.

People who ordinarily are polite in their personal lives, and maybe even attend church on a regular basis, let loose with the foulest language. The four-letter words fly over the Internet, as do the personal insults and threats. Anyone who runs an Internet marketing business, as I do (I sell information products at www.bly.com—click on Products from the main menu) knows this to be a fact of doing business on the Web.

Why do ordinarily civil folk turn into raving maniacs online? My guess is that the anonymity people enjoy on the Internet— often you don't know their name when they comment on a blog, and certainly they never have to confront you in person or over the phone—brings them a dose of "courage" that they frankly wouldn't have if they were talking to you face-to-face.

While I am all for honesty, I was also raised in an older generation, the baby boomers, where people were expected to show respect for one another. On the Internet, that has largely disappeared.

I've seen this numerous times. For instance, my e-newsletter has an unsubscribe feature, but technology being the mystery that it is, the unsubscribe feature does not always work reliably.

And on occasion, someone who thought they unsubscribed gets, despite our best efforts, another issue.

Now, you wouldn't think this was a crime on par with, say, Auschwitz. After all, if I get something in my e-mail in-box that I don't want, it takes me less than a second and just a click of the mouse to delete it forever.

But other people apparently don't feel that way. I have received lengthy e-mails from people who unsuccessfully unsubscribed and received another issue of my e-zine, in which they threaten legal action, question my intelligence, and rant on for paragraphs.

Some of the messages are short. Just the other day, a fellow named Dale, whom I've never met, sent me an e-mail with a single line: "Just remove us from your #%&*$ list."

Nice, especially considering I didn't spam him; the *only* way to get on my list is to sign up for it.

So it seems to me that, on blogs, anything goes, and you can say anything—except, apparently, saying that blogs aren't the greatest thing since sliced bread. That, I've learned, is taboo.

"Here is another reason to be wary of blogs," says a well-known online marketing expert who asked not to be named for fear of reprisal from the blogosphere. "The tone of some of these messages is so nasty and intemperate, that I can't imagine anyone in a corporation wanting to hire some of these people after taking a look at their blog.

"It's like recording your gossip sessions and broadcasting them worldwide. This is not private, and on the Internet it's forever." And if not forever, it's at least beyond your control: content I have taken off my Web site has been found in Google long after I removed it from my server.

RULE 7:
The blogosphere considers itself
exempt from the normal rules of conversational
etiquette and polite behavior as practiced in all
other forms of communication, including
conversation and e-mail.

Is selling yourself, your company, or your product acceptable in the blogosphere?

Blogging began with a noble purity: free and open conversation about virtually any topic, available to all at no charge on the Internet.

The Internet, as you know, began with a similar noble purity: an efficient, fast medium for communication and dissemination of technical information by the scientific research community.

Any time there is a new technology, the users generally fall into two camps: those who just want to enjoy it and think it should be free, and those who want to "monetize" it—in other words, make money from it.

Many years ago, selling online was considered blasphemy. The Internet was seen as a channel of communication, not a channel for commerce. There was a widespread belief that everything on the Internet should be free.

Today, of course, the Internet has completely revolutionized marketing as we know it. Billions of dollars of goods, services, and content are sold online each year. And the Internet has in many cases proven itself to be many times more cost-effective than TV, radio, magazine advertising, and printed direct mail.

According to the U.S. Census Bureau, shoppers in the United States spent $29 billion in 2000. In the first three quarters of 2005 alone, total e-commerce sales in the United States were $59.7 billion.

It was inevitable that the monetizing of the Internet would spread to blogs. The question is: does permitting advertising or product promotion on a blog destroy the credibility of blogging?

Clearly, the blogosphere has accepted paid advertising on blogs, as long as it is clearly delineated as such. Many of the top blogging gurus feature banner ads, for their products as well as from advertisers, in the margins of their blogs. Joshua Marshall, a political blogger, says he makes five thousand dollars a month from banner ads on his blog.[1]

For several weeks, *ad*RANTS.com, my favorite advertising blog, had a banner ad at the top promoting a landing page guide from *MarketingSherpa*. The *Sherpa* people obviously paid for the ad, and they wouldn't have done so week after week unless it was making money for them.

As for promoting a product within the text of the blog itself, while that has been traditionally frowned upon, acceptance of product talk in blogs is slowly growing.

In my opinion, whether and how much you can talk about products in a blog follows roughly the same 80/20 rule for balancing content versus product promotion in an e-newsletter: at least 80 and preferably 90 percent of the text must be pure content; 10 to 20 percent can promote products, either those of the e-newsletter publisher or products he or she recommends. Stick with 80/20 in your blog and your readers won't complain.

When you do mention products, it's best to do so within the context of the editorial content of your e-newsletter or blog.

For instance, let's say you write a gardening blog. You are telling the reader how you grew prize-winning roses, and part of your method involves using a specific brand of fertilizer. Naturally, your readers want to know what brand that is, so you are doing them a service by naming it. Your readers may also want to order some, so you are doing them a service by putting a link from your blog to the manufacturer's Web site, where they can place an order for the fertilizer.

Now, if that's all you've done, it's not really advertising; it's more of an "editorial mention." But what if you have an affiliate arrangement with the fertilizer manufacturer so that you get a percentage of all sales generated by traffic to their site that comes from the link in your blog?

If you publish an e-zine like I do, and your subscriber list is fairly large, you will be inundated with e-mail correspondence from e-book publishers—and other online marketers—asking you to promote their product to your list on an "affiliate basis."

In the affiliate arrangement, you—the e-zine owner—get a commission on every sale generated by the promotion to your list, typically ranging from 25 to 50 percent of the product price. The product can be promoted in a solo e-mail marketing message to the e-zine subscriber list or an online ad in the e-zine itself—or both.

These kinds of "affiliate deals" are done all the time in Internet marketing, particularly through affiliate links in e-newsletters. Why not do affiliate promotions through your blog?

The reason, one could argue, is that you would be allowing advertisers to influence the content and message of your blog, which the reader assumes is pure, unadulterated editorial free of promotional messages.

Or do they assume that? On my blog, I once asked the question, "Is the e-zine publisher obligated to disclose to the reader that he is an affiliate for the product and will receive a cut of the sale?"

I thought my blog readers would say yes, but they didn't. The consensus was this: Internet users are sophisticated enough these days to know that people who "own" or control Web traffic deserve to profit from that traffic, as long as they don't abuse ethical and legal standards—for example, allow spam to be sent to their list or lie in their content to sell a product.

Whether you publish an e-newsletter, a content-rich Web site, or a blog, you go to a lot of time, trouble, and expense to produce that information, which readers are getting free. Readers understand that they are getting your material free, and therefore don't object to your making some money to compensate you for your effort—at least, that's what I think.

Putting direct links to useful resources for readers, by the way, is one area where the Internet is much more "with it" than newspapers and other mainstream media.

This stems from a tradition in newspaper publishing to remain objective and not seem to be promoting any company or product.

Therefore, I frequently find an article in my local daily newspaper here in northern New Jersey that mentions a book or product I'd like to order, but to my frustration, gives no contact information for the publisher or manufacturer. How stupid!

On the Internet, you can rest assured that if a blog or e-newsletter publisher was talking about a book or product, they'd put a hyperlink in their review or article. The reader can get more product detail or place an order just by clicking on that link.

A newspaper publisher or editor might think this is cheap salesmanship, but in today's busy world, it's a service and convenience I, as a reader, want. Blogs and e-newsletters give it to me; many print media don't.

Another trend toward the commercialization of blogs is companies hiring bloggers to blog about the company or their products or technology. Readers seem to accept this practice provided the bloggers clearly explain their relationship with the sponsor on the blog and the sponsor does not influence or edit what is written on the blog. Software publisher Marqui hired more than a dozen bloggers to mention Marqui at least once a week on their blogs, in return for which they were paid an eight-hundred-dollar flat fee per week, plus an additional fifty dollars for every qualified sales lead sent to Marqui from their blog.[2]

Meanwhile, Guinness, the brewer, recently launched a Weblog. It is written by Guinness staffers, and not the brewer's ad agency, a move praised in the *ad*RANTS ad blog, which notes: "Many blogs written by agencies for clients just don't seem to gel." The reason, according to *ad*RANTS, is that the closer the commentary is to the humans creating the voice, the more authentic and credible the blog.[3]

Using copyrighted material in your blog

I've noticed bloggers frequently using what appears to be copyrighted material—mainly photos, cartoons, and other images—in their blogs. In several cases, I e-mailed the blogger asking if the material was in fact copyrighted and whether he or she had obtained the copyright holder's permission to use it.

In each case, the blogger's answer was, "No, I guess it's wrong, but I'm really not hurting anybody, and after all, I'm only a lone blogger, not a giant corporation, so what's the harm? And besides, I am really helping the creator, giving his work a broader exposure and possibly generating increased sales for him."

Because of the now-fading-but-still-pervading belief that "content on the Internet should be free," many Internet users in general and bloggers in particular are casual about using copyrighted material in their own Web sites and electronic publications.

But if you use or download copyrighted digital content without paying for it—music, movies, books, articles—you're stealing from the creator of the material, pure and simple.

An article in *BusinessWeek* announced that Google is planning to scan the complete texts of millions of books from major libraries around the world and make them searchable online.

"Problem No. 1 is that Google's plan is a clear violation of copyright laws," reports *BusinessWeek*. The article quotes Peter Givler, executive director of the Association of American University Presses, who notes that the Google plan "appears to involve systematic infringement of copyright on a massive scale."

As an author, I am outraged. What Google is doing is not much different than raiding a farmer's field at night, harvesting all the crops, and giving it away to hungry people—without paying the farmer a dime.

Forget "Citizen's Publishing." If you want to give away your work on the Internet for free, that's your business.

But if you take my copyrighted work and post it on your site without my permission, you're a thief—and, like any thief, you should be punished if caught.

Recently, writer Harlan Ellison sued AOL, claiming that they did not act fast enough in removing a copyrighted story of his that a user had illegally posted online.

"There is a culture of belief today that everything should be free," says Ellison. "The Internet is the glaring promoter of such slacker-gen 'philosophy,' and that goes to the core of my lawsuit.

"People have been gulled into believing that everything should be free, and that if a professional gets published, well, any thief can steal it, and post it, and the thug feels abused if you whack him for it.

"Meanwhile, vast hordes of semi- or untalented amateurs

festoon the Internet with their ungrammatical, puerile trash, and they think because this 'vanity' publication gets seen by a few people, that they are 'writers.' Horse puckey!

"That isn't being published; that's the fanzine press. And there are fewer and fewer real venues for a professional writer nowadays to make a decent living at the craft," explains Ellison.

"I'll go to speak at a college, and I'll have some kid stand up and say, 'Well, writers shouldn't be paid; they should put their stuff up; and if people like it they get paid for it.' And I think: what looneytune universe are you *living* in, kid? The question indicates a total lack of understanding of how reality works. This kid's been living off mommy and daddy too long.

"Or someone else will say you ought to be subsidized, and I say, well, the last time I looked, the doge of Venice or the pope wasn't laying out much green to keep the mortgage paid or food on the table of American storytellers. So until a wealthy and generous patron decides that I'm worth subsidizing, I'll have to scrabble in the bean field just like everybody else."

There's a growing movement among some folks to make all information in the world available to everyone on the planet at no charge. But if information is free to consumers, that means the salaries of the subject-matter experts, writers, and editors whose job it is to produce content must all be paid by advertising, rather than subscription and product sales.

One can argue that all content producers would then be influenced by advertisers, who would hold their financial fate in their hands. Content producers who produce objective, unbiased reporting because they accept no advertising, like traditional subscription newsletter publishers, cannot survive if they must give away everything they produce for free.

And the next time you want to use copyrighted material without paying for it, whether posting a cartoon on your blog or watching a movie, think of my friend Bob.

"I was a singer-songwriter who had an 'artistic development' deal in Nashville during 2001 to 2002," Bob wrote me in a recent letter. "However, the music downloading issues of the past few years killed my Nashville deal. Much of the music industry was hit hard from this illegal activity. From 1999 to 2002, CD sales were down a staggering 30 percent."

According to an article in *BusinessWeek*, online thieves download 2.6 billion illegal music files and 12 million movies a month, costing the music and movie industries millions of dollars a year: "The problem is finding a way to protect copyright holders without blocking important innovations such as the iPod."

So let me ask: why are people who advocate Citizen's Publishing so dead set against business models where creators charge money—and get paid—for fiction, journalism, music, art, and other content?

Why should "content be free," as so many Internet enthusiasts insist, while people in all other professions, from plumbers to psychotherapists, get paid for their expertise, talents, and efforts?

Most consumers, by the way, don't buy into this "all information is free" lie, and if you bought this book, neither do you. According to an article in *BtoB*, the information industry will generate revenues of $306 billion in 2006. That's an increase of 8 percent over 2005 sales—an indicator that the growing presence of the Internet is stimulating rather than retarding the sale of paid content.

Oh yes, in August 2005, Google announced that the company was temporarily suspending its program to scan copyrighted books from large university libraries. But rather than seek permission to scan specific books, they wanted to require publishers to contact Google and let them know which copyrighted books the publisher doesn't want scanned.

Here's something Google seems to have overlooked in their original plan to scan old books in the world's biggest university libraries: once a book goes out of print, all rights typically revert to the author. And as far as I can see, Google has made no mention of determining whether a book is in print and, if so, tracking down the author for permission. So they would essentially be violating the copyright of authors whose books are out of print.

Now, when I said as much on my blog, bloggers took me to task. They explained to me, as if speaking to a slow child, that Google scanning my out-of-print books and making them available online would actually spark sales of the actual book. Well, if the book is out of print, then the only way you can get it is to buy a used copy—and while that's nice for the author, he doesn't make a royalty on sales of secondhand books.

But, I was told, the availability of my old titles on Google would spark interest in my newer books as well, and so I would stand to make money on those sales, and was foolish to object to Google's plans.

Here's what they missed: whether offering my copyrighted material in a different format or venue is good for me or not is irrelevant. The point is that it is copyrighted material to which I, not Google or anyone else, own the rights. Therefore, the decision to offer it in any format or venue is strictly the author's, and if he doesn't want electronic versions of his old books online, that's his business, whether you think it's a good decision or not.

RULE 7a:
Copyright laws apply everywhere, offline and online, including the blogosphere: just because you aren't selling your blog content doesn't mean you can post copyrighted material belonging to others without their permission.

Blogging, *The Cluetrain Manifesto*, and "conversation"

For simplicity, the marketing world can be divided into two distinct segments: (1) image advertising or "branding" and (2) direct marketing.

It's my observation that in the marketing world, blogging evangelists are almost all from the branding side of marketing rather than direct marketing.

I have also noticed that branding people are absolutely in love with the book *The Cluetrain Manifesto*. Yet this book almost never appears on any direct marketer's list of important marketing books to read.

Therefore, if you read marketing blogs, *The Cluetrain Manifesto* comes up frequently and, when it does, is always discussed in reverent, worshipful tones—as if it is the "Bible" of marketing, and its teaching beyond dispute or question.

But I think, to some degree, *The Cluetrain Manifesto* is a load of horse hooey. And anyone who takes it seriously as their marketing bible is off their rocker.

Here's why: by proclaiming that "markets are conversations," and that talking with customers is the ultimate marketing methodology, *Cluetrain* ignores this important truism from Rene Descartes: "To know what people really think, pay regard to what they do, rather than what they say."

That's where we direct marketers have it all over the *Cluetrain* crowd. We aren't guided just by what people say they want or will do; we primarily pay attention to what they actually do—in other words, what they buy.

You can determine what your prospects will buy based on your own test mailing—or by studying the successful control mailings of your competitors in the same category.

Because those control mailings are working, they tell you the appeals that are causing customers to open their wallets—those marketing approaches that are making money right now.

Actions speak louder than words, and what people actually buy is infinitely more important than what they say they will buy.

Which do you think is a more accurate indicator of what your market wants—a "conversation" or a purchase?

Now, while I don't agree with a lot of what is in *The Cluetrain Manifesto*, its advice on writing *style* is useful for copywriting and also for blogging.

For years, the first rule of copywriting—especially direct-marketing copy—has been, "Write in a natural, conversational style."

And *Cluetrain* tells us: "Conversations among human beings sound human. They are conducted in a human voice. The human voice is typically open, natural, uncontrived."

I couldn't agree more. But here's the weird thing: most

branding and marketing consultants I encounter in the blogosphere worship *The Cluetrain Manifesto.* Yet they totally ignore its advice on writing style.

RULE 8:
Bloggers consider conversation, not selling, to be the most effective form of marketing products and services online. That sounds politically correct, but it doesn't reflect reality.

Why corporations are afraid of blogging: the Kryptonite story

By now I'm sure you've heard of the Kryptonite story, in which bloggers revealed a fundamental flaw in the Kryptonite company's lock that did huge damage to their reputation and sales.

Here's what happened: A blogger posted an item explaining that the Kryptonite lock could easily be picked with a ballpoint pen. Other bloggers and the mainstream media, including the Associated Press and the *New York Times*, picked up on the story.

Technorati estimates that within one week of the original post, 1.8 million people had read postings about the Kryptonite lock. A few days later, the manufacturer announced it would exchange any affected locks for free, at an estimated cost of $10 million, the equivalent of 40 percent of the company's $25 million annual revenues.

And then there's the infamous Dell customer who, frustrated with what he thought was poor customer service bashed Dell continually in his widely read blog.

Based on these incidents, blogging evangelists and consultants felt they had their proof that blogs were indeed the next revolution in marketing.

But as far as I can see, with rare exception, blogs have not made a major contribution to the average company's ROMD.

I am not saying that both individuals and corporations haven't gotten value from their blogs—quite the contrary. But in each case, the blog is a supplementary, and largely secondary, component of an overall marketing strategy.

The blog is never the major generator of revenues, as e-mail marketing is for Agora Publishing, a newsletter publisher from whom e-mail marketing generates more than $100 million in annual revenue, or as a Web site is for Blue Nile, which sells millions of dollars worth of diamonds and diamond jewelry online every year.

Based on the Kryptonite and Dell incidents, it would seem that a more important aspect of blogs as they relate to marketing is damage control: what to do if a customer, employee, or vendor attacks you or your product on their blog.

This is an area in which retaining a blogging consultant is a worthwhile investment: negative PR on blogs not under one's direct control is a relatively new phenomenon, and most marketing managers have no experience or expertise in this area.

So what's the use of a blog? And in what way is it acceptable to use your blog to make money or otherwise further your business, career, or other interests?

In *The Weblog Handbook: Practical Advice on Creating and Maintaining Your Blog*, Rebecca Blood writes:

Individuals whose Weblogs focus on a particular topic become known as experts in their field. Providing a reliable resource for news about a certain topic is enough to gain you a dependable following among fellow professionals or aficionados. If you take the time to frame this information with your own remarks, you may be regarded as insightful and informed. If your subject matter tends to be particularly esoteric, you may gain a reputation that leads to employment, speaking engagements, and even book contracts.

Freelancers and small business owners can raise their profile by creating and maintaining a Weblog that focuses on their field of expertise. Sharing information is one of the best ways to gain respect in any field. Once you would have had to publish a book or magazine article or speak at professional events, and these opportunities were rare unless you had already achieved a certain prominence. The Web has circumvented all the gate-keepers, and now everyone with a Webpage has the means to reach an audience of like-minded individuals. A business wishing to build or leverage the existing reputations of its staff may want to publish a collaborative Weblog in which each person contributes and comments on topical links.

If you hope to convert this prominence into actual revenue, focus on the needs of your customers. A plumber who maintains a Weblog focused on the latest pipe fittings may acquire a devout audience of other plumbers, but this may not translate so readily into sinks to unclog. But if her Weblog also includes information to help the homeowner troubleshoot minor plumbing snafus . . . it may also help attract and keep loyal customers. Customers like to feel that they are dealing with trusted experts; your Weblog can be your calling card.[4]

Bad blogging: the "bloatosphere"

Note: The following is contributed by Steven Streight, president and CEO of Streight Site Systems. His company specializes in Web research, user observation testing, usability analysis, Web creditability enhancement, content writing, and business blogs. He also writes computer books.

The "bloatosphere" is the realm of blogs that is becoming bloated or fattened by the rapid accumulation of anti-blogs: broadcast blogs, pseudo-blogs, simulated blogs, drivel blogs, link blogs, fictional persona blogs, and link farm blogs.

"Broadcast blogs" are blogs that, by not being interactive—that is, by not enabling users to post comments to the blogger—violate the primary purpose of blogging, which is starting a candid, intimate conversation with a larger audience.

Some bloggers will not enable comments due to comment spam problems. Today I had to change my settings on one of my blogs because I got hit with eight comment spams and had to manually search the comments of sixty-seven posts to find and delete them. Now users must register if they want to post a comment on my "Vaspers the Grate" site.

"Unilateral blogs" are not all bad and may be appropriate for certain situations. But they really are not blogs; they're quasi-blog bulletin boards.

"Pseudo-blogs" (also known as "proxy-blogs") are blogs created by ad agencies or marketing professionals who charge a sucker, I mean, client, to design, ghostwrite, maintain, and promote it.

It is "pseudo" because the voice posting is not the authentic, candid, personal voice of the alleged blog author, but rather a hired hand. Thus it is definitely *not* a real blog and never can be, unless the client fires the ghost-blogger and starts posting his own thoughts in his own words.

It is acceptable practice to help a client compose posts, to edit them, or to write some sample posts just to show the client how to do it. But to ghost-blog, this is not authentic or credible. Others may disagree, but I see no good reasons for ghost-blogging. If a CEO can't blog, he should find someone in the firm who can, who knows the industry, products, and customers well.

As an article in *ad*RANTS observes: "Many blogs created/produced/written by agencies for clients just don't seem to gel. It's not that every client-created blog will either, but the closer the blog is to the humans creating the voice, the truer and more realistic the blog will sound."[5]

A hired blogger who blogs about topics related to the company and its products is acceptable and not in the same class as a genuine "pseudo blog." In this case, the professional blogger is not pretending to be the client, is not putting words into the client's mouth. For example, I could see an amateur astronomer-blogger hired to write a blog for a telescope manufacturer, as long as he writes in his own persona and doesn't pretend to be the CEO.

However, if the ghost-blogger from outside the company and industry, who has no real passion for the product, is being paid to say nice things about the company and its products, it fills my head with question marks. It seems disingenuous, phony. If ghost-blogs become popular and pervasive, we will grow to be skeptical about all the blogs we encounter. "Is this really Bill Gates, or is it someone he paid to speak for him?"

And if a ghost-blogger writes on behalf of a CEO, users are being tricked into interacting with a phony. Isn't that what consumers dislike about much advertising, direct mail, and celebrity endorsements?

Aren't we moving closer to consumer fraud when we accept proxy blogging? Consumer: "He doesn't really use and love the product. He's getting paid big bucks to pretend he does, but actually it's a lie."

"Ghost-blogging"—writing blog posts for a client—takes place because the client:

1. Can't write
2. Is stupid or inept
3. Has a fear of blogging
4. Hates having to learn new skills, so delegates or out-sources the blogging to others
5. Just sells product but doesn't know anything about the industry or customers, thus literally cannot blog about it
6. Refuses to spend the time required to learn how to blog but thinks "should have a blog" since it's the trendy thing to do
7. Has been persuaded by the ad guys or marketing hacks that they can do a better job writing the blog posts, since they allegedly "specialize in communication, branding, and customer relations."

"Simulated blogs" are fake blogs that a company sponsors just because it is considered the trendy thing to do, and their ad agency or marketing team is desperate to come up with some device to make the client think they still have some value. Many have no regular posting, no author, no interactivity, no links, no conventional blog features.

"Drivel blogs" are personal blogs that are poorly written and designed, have no value except for catharsis and narcissistic self-expression for the blog author, and are usually abandoned after the author realizes no one cares or comments.

I'm not referring to digital journals, where a person is striving to keep track of items, to improve their writing skills, or to provide entertainment for friends and family.

When I say "drivel," I mean egotistic personal blogs that are created just to blabber pointlessly, sloppily recording trivial, mundane events and feelings, with no value to self or others. These are like phone calls or visits from a person who chatters endlessly and annoyingly about his or her self and expresses no interest in you.

"Drivel blogging" can infect a business blog when business topics are buried in excessive amounts of irrelevant personal details. Be careful with adding personal details to a business blog. Don't let private revelations distract users from the more important material on your blog.

"Sleazy link blogs" are blogs created to incorporate links for, and drive traffic to, sleazy sites devoted to dubious, fraudulent, or malicious online gambling, online pharmacies, low-rate loan sharks, sexual-enhancement products, bogus computer products and software, con artist pseudo-charities, charlatan diet aids, etc.

"Fictional persona blogs" are phony blogs of nonexistent characters who are deceptively writing about imaginary events involving other make-believe characters, fantasy adventures, and pretended musings about a customer base or product.

If a company has a branded fictional persona blogging for them (e.g., Ronald McDonald, Barney, the Chicken of the Sea tuna mermaid, the Pillsbury doughboy), this may not be entirely bad practice, but consider the ramifications carefully. Why should you want to deliver your marketing message via a false entity? Is the CEO really that unknown or uninteresting?

"Link farm blogs" are unreal, artificial blogs created simply to link to a target site, to boost its search engine and link popularity rank.

RULE 8a:
To be effective marketing vehicles, blogs should be relatively free of marketing. They should contain useful content and the truth, not hype or sales talk. To violate this rule not only costs you sales and credibility, but it also incurs the disdain and wrath of the blogosphere.

CHAPTER 4

POLITICAL BLOGGING

Though many people refuse to talk politics, they don't seem to have the same hesitation when it comes to writing about the subject. According to two studies conducted in early 2005 by the Pew Internet & American Life Project, blogs have firmly established themselves as a key part of our online culture.

Eleven million people—or one out of every seventeen Americans—have created a blog. And their writing isn't going unnoticed. The Pew study confirms the explosion of blogging. According to the study, thirty-two million Americans read blogs and another 12 percent post comments or other material on the sites. In 2004, blog readership jumped 58 percent from the previous year.

But are laws, issues, and candidates really the hot topics being buzzed on the Internet? Although writer Jorn Barger coined the term "blog" in 1997, it wasn't until 1999 that blogs began to take off.

A recent Google search for "political blogs" turned up 18.7 million hits in nineteen seconds. Clearly, people are talking about the affairs of their local communities, their states, their country, and the leaders in charge of all of them.

RULE 9:

If your goal in blogging is not mere self-expression but to influence others, the type of blog you should write (in order of influence) should be political, technology, or business.

The roots of political blogging

After September 11, 2001, Americans found themselves in a state of disbelief that they'd been attacked on home soil. As shell-shocked as we were, we heeded the age-old belief that if we could just talk about what happened, we just might begin to feel better.

Over the ensuing weeks and months, we found ourselves not only watching continous television coverage, listening to radio talk shows, and reading endless articles about every aspect of the terrorists' actions and our own reactions, but we also turned to each other—through the Internet.

On March 20, 2003, the first full day of hostilities in Iraq, Alan Nelson, a full-time management consultant and part-time blogger, and Michele Catalano founded The Command Post. Nelson described it as a public service/news resource published by a group of bloggers from around the world trying to post the latest professional news they'd seen, heard, or read.

The Command Post's mission statement promised to offer readers a deep range of global news sources on a narrow range of topics and to give them an opportunity to "triangulate" the media on specific news topics and to provide a forum in which readers could offer varying perspectives through civil and respectful comments and dialogue. In exchange, Nelson and Catalano hoped to advance blogging to a state of open source citizen journalism and reward their contributors by increasing awareness of individual Weblogs.

Within four days, the 120 bloggers initially involved with The Command Post had quickly used up their space on Blogspot's server. Within two months, the blog had two million visitors including ordinary readers and professional journalists.

By August 2004, The Command Post boasted a roster of 166 bloggers with posting privileges and lives as diverse as their opinions. From a Manhattan attorney whose law office was located in the World Trade Center to a Vietnam veteran whose hobby is chasing tornadoes and a Ph.D. candidate who admits he blogs to avoid writing his dissertation, each also has a home blog that readers of The Command Post are encouraged to visit.

Clearly, a lot of folks had—and continue to have—a lot to say about the state of our country and world affairs. As the Internet grew along with Americans' need for instant news, we turned our attention to the fledgling world of blogs, which provided the perfect vehicle to rant, rave, discuss, and debate.

After the invasion of Afghanistan, bloggers increased their discussion of rapidly changing world events. Glenn Reynolds, a distinguished law professor at the University of Tennessee, furthered the popularity of blogging in 2001 when he created Instapundit, a site that began as an experiment in his Internet law class and has grown into one of the world's most widely read political blogs in existence today.

Warblogs, a term created by Matt Welch, former associate editor and media columnist for *Reason* magazine, mainly discussed the war on terror, but gradually he and other bloggers branched out into peripheral territories that included politics and the cultural and social issues being affected by the government's military actions and policies.

Initially, the majority of warblogs was conservative in nature and supported the United States' war policies. On September 17, 2001, Welch posted the following entry on the warblog he created:

Welcome to War. Sounds like a strange and unpleasant thing to say, but these are strange and unpleasant times, requiring unusual responses. Like many of you, I am reading and hearing and watching too much about the wicked horror of Sept. 11, and finding it a challenge to keep track of how it is already changing our lives.

The biggest question facing Americans and other decent people is how the civilized world and its strongest country should respond to this mass murder. I, for one, advocate a Global War to abolish terrorism. Many of you probably disagree. There are—largely thanks to the values championed by the United States—many forums to argue over the many issues that are already cropping up, from concerns over reduced civil liberties to an amazing increase in government secrecy. This will be mine . . . and yours too, should you want to e-mail me and agree to let me share it with the others.

There aren't many who can think and write clearly in the wake of this terrible sadness, and I don't claim to be one of them, but I will try. This site will also be a press review, allowing you and me both to monitor and react to coverage and opinion as it happens. I had always hoped to conduct my affairs without resorting to the blog, but new times call for new media. Let's roll.

An eye toward politics

When formal military operations ceased, the focus of war-blogs changed yet again. Instead of just discussing the war on terror, bloggers turned their attention to politics in general. According to Welch, political blogging has provided the missing link in speeding up the news cycle to one second instead of the traditional twenty-four hours or once-a-week news updates Americans have been accustomed to.

"In addition to having outlets like the Drudge Report, blogs have forced traditional media to become re-acquainted with its round-the-clock news cycle," Welch says. "Now, if enough bloggers decide that X is a story, X will be covered by the traditional media, without exception. We saw this during the last election cycle especially with the Swift Boat story and the Dan Rather memo story."

Blogging opened up the concept of citizen journalism by providing the vehicle for ordinary folks to express their opinions through a creative medium that had no official standards in which to judge and little regulation to halt the freedom of their speech.

"The line between what some bloggers do and the art of journalism is getting very hard to define," says John Sullivan, who frequently writes about ethics and politics on his blog and is an avid reader of countless other sites. "Some bloggers were given press passes at the Democratic and Republican 2004 conventions, so how do you differentiate? The term 'blog' is getting to be a pretty stretched-out term that applies to a lot of different things."

As word about specific blogs spread, people from both the Left and the Right realized they'd found virtual groups where support could be bolstered and disagreements aired. According to Dave Johnson, an MSNBC hardblogger and founder of Seeing the Forest, a credentialed Weblog at the 2004 Democratic National Convention, "Blogs operate as an 'open source think tank' where ideas are expressed on one blog and discussed in the comments that are posted. Then another blog links to it and comments, the first blog responds, etc."

Blogging is a process, says Johnson, which allows ideas to be processed at an extremely rapid rate. "Blogs have provided the informed activists with a way to express their views and get those views in front of party leaders."

As the 2004 presidential election neared, journalists, pundits, and residents of future red and blue states were quick to recognize the advantage of the instantaneity of the Internet. Intelliseek's BlogPulse Campaign Radar 2004 Web site tracked and analyzed political blog content daily from more than two million blogs.

BlogPulse found the Drudge Report, Glenn Reynolds's Instapundit, and Markos Moulitsas Zuniga's DailyKos were the sites most bloggers turned to and referenced in their political postings. Though the report revealed Iraq was the most often referred to topic, it was closely followed by opinions about the economy, health care, the environment, and education—all subjects of interest to aspiring and established political candidates.

In a press release dated October 24, 2004, Intelliseek's

CMO Pete Blackshaw stated that, "clearly, bloggers' influence on political discussion and the election is evident and growing. The Web-enabled public is relying on a variety of sources, including blogs, traditional media, and other Web sites to inform themselves, find unfiltered opinions, and to guide their votes. And bloggers, in some instances, are pushing the envelope in defining the political agenda and news coverage."

While bloggers were busy getting the word out, political parties and their candidates were assessing the information and using it as part of their strategic planning for winning elections. According to Dave Johnson, while Howard Dean's candidacy was credited with using blogs to communicate out, a very important use of blogs in Dean's early campaign was bringing information in.

"They were reading blogs and becoming aware of the huge disconnect between the Democratic Party's base and its leadership in Washington on most issues," Johnson says. "This information provided the realization that led to Dean's ability to voice what the 'base' was thinking, and propelled him to his surprising lead until Iowa."

As bloggers continued to express their thoughts and opinions, they were also beginning to see even more ways to have an impact on the political scene. Many groups became enmeshed with political parties and "527" groups whose clout expanded to party fund-raisers.

Candidates and their parties set up blogs to get their agendas in front of a voting America. "One of the main effects blogging has had on national politics is by becoming a very influential, high-speed and deep-pocketed fundraising tool," says *Reason*'s Matt Welch. "The reason why Howard Dean is the chairman of the Democratic Party is that his campaign was able to raise vast sums of money and generate vast sums of excitement using the Internet and Web blogs."

In the fall of 2003, Howard Dean's campaign raised $7.4 million through the Internet. The money raised didn't come from a few large donors but through many smaller donations averaging around one hundred dollars.

The Bush and Kerry campaigns also launched Web sites to boost their grassroots efforts, but they were not credited with having the impact that Dean's site did. Senator John Kerry's blog with 1,616 links ranked twenty-second out of the top one hundred political blogs while President Bush's blog with 581 links ranked fiftieth.

"There were many complaints about the blogs started by the individual campaigns," says blogger follower John Sullivan. "Some people believe they cherry-picked which comments to approve for posting and that gave it the pretense of having an open discussion. In that way, they functioned like the town hall meetings we saw on television during the elections where both the audience and the questions were pre-screened without everyone realizing that was the case. I'm sure there will be a big emphasis on that sort of thing with party blogs in the next election cycle."

Whether preplanned or not, political blogs in general complemented the traditional media and in some cases went a step further and broke headline stories first or quickly fact-checked stories as they were hitting the news service wires. One clear example comes from the first bloggers who linked to the Swift Boat Veterans for Truth and their anti-Kerry video that emerged in late July 2004.

Determined to expose what they deemed to be true, these bloggers refused to let the subject go and didn't let up until Kerry and the mainstream media responded. Similarly, Power Line, a blog created by John Hinderaker, Scott Johnson, and Paul Mirengoff, broke the story about President Bush's supposed preferred treatment in the Air National Guard.

Power Line refused to let up until Dan Rather, the CBS newsman who stood by the story, admitted the documents were fake and apologized later in the month. Power Line recorded the highest number of citations on a single day regarding the alleged forged documents.

Blogs definitely worked for Ben Chandler, a Kentucky Democratic congressional candidate, whose campaign was the first of several to start advertising on political blogs. His campaign invested two thousand dollars in blog advertising and got an eighty-thousand-dollar return in less than two weeks— mostly in donations that ranged from twenty to eighty dollars.

Chandler went on to win a seat in the House of Representatives. Since then, in an effort to regulate paid advertising on the Internet, the Federal Election Commission is considering rules that would apply federal campaign finance regulations to online speech.

Young people in particular increasingly get their news not from newspapers or television but from blogs and other online sources. Merrill Brown, the founding editor-in-chief of MSNBC, said, "The future of the U.S. news industry is seriously threatened by the seemingly irrevocable move by young people away from traditional media sources."

Jesse Oxfeld, online editor of *Editor & Publisher*, observes that blogs and other online sources often take news from mainstream sources, repeat it, and then analyze or comment on the news. But "the actual reporting of that news, from which all the analysis and watchdogging and bloggery and so forth arises, is still largely done by those same old traditional news outlets [which] still costs a lot of money."[1]

He then poses the question: if young people get their news from blogs and other online sources, and don't read newspapers, who will pay for original reporting, which will always cost a lot of money? Working independently, individual news and political bloggers, most of whom have full-time day jobs in other areas, can't even begin to match the investigative resources of major newspapers and newsmagazines.

Becoming a political blogger

Do you need to be politically and Internet savvy in order to find quality blog material—or to start your own blog or contribute to an established site?

Dave Johnson says DailyKos and Eschaton are two popular blogs that are influential because of the number of readers they have. "Of course the readership reflects the writing, but some blogs are saying things that are not as interesting to wide audiences as to Party insiders, and those blogs have been receiving recognition as well," he adds.

For the everyday reader looking to become more political savvy, Matt Welch suggests doing a Google search on what elements of politics are of interest to you. From there, if you like what you're reading, start clicking on the permanent links and bookmark those you find interesting.

"I guarantee you'll find twenty interesting blogs on whatever interests you within twenty-four hours," Welch says. As for what determines if the blog you're reading is believable or well written, Welch adds, "That would depend on a little something called 'your personal judgment.'"

If you're pressed for time, you'll want to find the "A-list" blogs—the ones most people deem worth reading. A Google search for "blog directory" returns 2.24 million hits in nineteen seconds. That includes Blogarama, which bills itself as "the" blog directory.

Blogarama provides eighty-five links to the liberal Left and thirty-seven links to sites for the conservative Right. Another site, Blogwise, hosts a total of 50,500 blogs with an average of 5,000 added each week. It bills itself as a site that has developed an "efficient, quick, and nice" portal to blogs around the world.

Pundit Memo, hosted by Blogger.com, describes itself as "commentary and analysis on today's politics, foreign policy, culture, and blogs—having fun, encouraging dialogue, and attempting to be savvy." Its founder, Kai Smith, is an honors student at Seattle University where he is pursuing majors in political science and history.

As the Internet continues to expand and news becomes faster to get, the future of political blogging looks big and bright. Says Dave Johnson: "Today people primarily hear about blogs through friends. And it is the reader that determines if they like what the blog says. If lots of readers agree with and enjoy what a blog is doing, they'll come back and the readership grows. Mass media sources also refer to a few already well-known blogs, and that also increases readership. It is the nature of blogs that once you happen upon one you are led to others through the links."

By the time the presidential election rolls around in 2008,

politicos and pundits will have honed their online rhetoric even more. They'll poke, prod, and undoubtedly inflame already-sensitive issues, and their activities are sure to make their way to mainstream media.

As blogging grows in popularity, political parties will continue to find new ways to use the information they gather and dig deeper to find out what bloggers are really thinking. When asked if political parties pay attention to blogs, Matt Welch replies with an emphatic, "Yes, they do. But probably mostly in a fire-extinguishing way.

"For example, if many important blogs are saying something terrible about a certain candidate, it then becomes a problem that needs to be dealt with," adds Welch. "I don't think it has yet evolved to a place where, say, the Powers-That-Be at the Democratic or Republican Party headquarters wake up every day and say, 'I hope we're getting good press on Instapundit!'"

Actually, that day may already be here. In 2005 the White House officially admitted what is believed to be the first blogger into its daily press briefings. The blogger, Garrett Graff, is only twenty-three years old. He writes Fishbowl D.C., a blog covering the Beltway news media. His first post dealt with the shabby conditions in the briefing room.[2]

CHAPTER 5

THE VANITY PRESS OF
PERSONAL BLOGS

Blogs have become an active part of today's net culture. But what's the driving force behind these expressive content-driven Web sites? Why does someone bother to make one without peddling a product or wanting to get in touch with consumers?

"The principal reason to blog is because you have something to say," says blogging consultant Paul Chaney. "Blogs, due to their magnetizing effect on search engines, are a prime way to share information and readership.

"While the cadre of readers may be small, it is not really how many sets of eyeballs are reading your material that's important, but who those eyeballs belong to. Blogs are written by influencers, and it is often other influencers that read them."

A blog can seem like a waste of time to some since there is no guarantee readers will come and comment. Having a blog can seem like a chore when you account for maintaining it with new posts and an interesting layout. What could be worth that work?

Then again, who wouldn't want to publish themselves on the

Web with this megaphone of the media world? Who wouldn't want a free megaphone that reaches the entire world?

But blogging is more than just putting content up on the Web and hoping someone will read. With so many blog directories, updated lists of published blogs, author profile indexes, and RSS feeds, it becomes possible for the people who want to read your blog to find it. The development of a reading audience is what's so attractive about blogs; they are the starting point for "free-form" blog communities.

The feeling of being connected to a community is one of the primary functions of the Internet. It is a basic human need to not feel alone or isolated. That is why so many communication devices like pagers, cellular phones, and PDAs are so popular. The blog is the new media device of today; but it is so much more, because its applications seem endless.

Millions of Americans have started blogs. Most are ordinary folk, entrepreneurs, or businesspeople. A few are celebrities. In 2005, Rosie O'Donnell launched a blog she described as "the unedited rantings of a fat forty-two-year-old menopausal ex–talk show host married mother of four."[1] Other celebrities who have blogged include Fred Durst and Barbra Streisand.

What is a blog community?

What I mean by "free-form" is that these communities are not shaped by a Web forum, chat room, or billboard. These communities are not shaped by topic, location, or need other than the need to publish and the feeling of being connected.

Blog communities have no particular shape, no list, and no newsletter, although they function fluidly. The blog authors are connected to one another by being both a writer and a reader, which (as I will discuss below) is extremely common. Whenever I have asked a blogger why he or she continues to maintain a blog, I am told that it's because of the feedback received and the friends found in the community built around their blog.

These communities just spring up from the commenting, which has become a standard feature on blogs. It starts with a reader commenting, which makes the author engrossed as to why that person read their blog.

Obviously this person knows about blogging in order to find a blog. Through that person's name or profile page an author can find his or her blog. Authors find themselves reading their blog and learning about what they have in common with this strange blogger. Usually, the authors post a comment in kind.

Commenting on this other author's blog in return links the strange community chain that develops. Before long, authors have a dialog going on across their blogs as they try to keep up with their new friends' posts.

Even more links are created as the reading network expands with new commentators on the author's blog and on the blogs of already-established friends. One author may regularly read five blogs, another may read twenty, and yet another author may read only the most recent post of the recent commentator.

Members of the blog community can be as active as they want to be or take the community a step further by creating permanent lists of friends' blogs on their blog's sidebar. These communities provide support for all the members and keep them posting something new.

The development of communities at Blogger.com

For me and many others these blog communities started at Blogger.com, a creation of Pyra Labs now owned by the media giant Google. Blogger.com provides free blogging for all without banners or ads. The simple set-up program and easy-to-use control tools provided allow you to manipulate your blog as you wish.

Blogger.com helps the new blog author with everything he/she could need or want, like precreated simple layout designs and extensive "help" pages. If Blogger.com doesn't provide a certain feature that you want, it's relatively easy to take the initiative and add it to the html/css code that is open for manipulation at the blog author's leisure.

When blogger.com got started, blog authors weren't sure if the online public was reading their posts. Many made their e-mail address available, but not many readers had the habit of taking the time to log in to their e-mail account to send a message to the unknown author. Then, blogger.com came up with their commenting device.

They created and implemented a way for blog authors to have a post-your-comments link under each post published. Commentators didn't need to be registered bloggers, and they didn't need to give their names.

Instead, commentators could just click on the link and be taken to a text window to write a comment. That comment would be instantly published under the post to which they were responding.

"This device saved the blogging experience, because once you turned it on—one simple click mind you—you finally had the proof that people were in fact reading your blog," says blogger Linda Walker. "Those who left their Blogger.com ID name or 'handle' allowed me to look at their Blogger.com profile, which held a link to their own blog. This helped me complete the very first chain for my little community or network of blog authors."

Why read and comment?

In January 2005, BBC news reported that blog reading had exploded in the United States. From a poll taken in November 2004, the number of Americans regularly reading blogs shot up by 58 percent.

The BBC attributed this growth for the most part to the political blogs that popped up for the presidential election. But the news network was astounded to find such a big increase considering the fact that only 60 percent of Internet users know what a blog is.

Since reading and commenting on blogs is key to the continuation of blogs, why do people care to read the post of some stranger? However, asking this question is like asking why people read newspapers or magazines at all.

The plain fact of the matter is that if you like what the person has to say, you will find yourself listening, or reading in this case. Howard Stern is a great example of this odd situation: because some people can sympathize with, understand, and even support him, he has become one of the top paid radio personalities even though he is often rude and crude.

Commenting is just a side effect of the highly held belief in free speech in America coupled with a need to connect, which I mentioned earlier. Why do people call in to the Howard Stern show? They want to confirm that they enjoy the show, they want to disagree with Howard, or they want to make a suggestion.

It's extremely similar with blogs. Once a reader comes across a blog for the first time by chance or curiosity, he or she makes an opinion.

If the reader enjoys the post, he or she will keep coming back and will start commenting regularly, or perhaps make only one comment if the blog wasn't interesting or was even upsetting. Bad grammar, cursing, or unusual topics will not stop readers, because audiences vary so much in this country. Some people prefer the author who tells it straight in his own voice, much like Howard Stern.

The short answer to why people comment is that most people do it just because they can. Give people an option and some of them will take it.

The spark of blogging

What makes someone want to start blogging in the first place? There are many reasons, and many blog authors have more than one for starting up their own blog.

- Since blogs are based on posting text, a good number of the blog authors today are writers who want to publish their work on the Web. JP, author of Burnsizzlebleed, who says: "I started blogging because I have arrived at the point where I want other people to read my work . . . and blogging is easier than standing on the corner handing out leaflets."

- Kathryn, who writes A Wolf Howl from My Mountain, says she started it from a purely professional standpoint, even though her blog has become a personal one: "I started my blog because an agent at a writer's conference said if writers were not blogging, they were missing a big opportunity to create a 'fan base' of future readers."

■ Shelly, who authors multiple writing blogs including Presto Speaks & Cyber Chocolate says, "I blog because I can." Being a writer and an artistic person, it was only natural that she try blogging. She enjoys creating the blogs, and filling them seems to be no problem for her.

Writers are the ones who started the whole blogging idea. Political and news writers began posting their thoughts on the Web in the style of an editor's column or log. These people are a mix of personal and business bloggers.

The only personal news writers I could mention here are the "old school" Web-surfer news writers. These are writers who are normally surfing the Web on a constant basis. Once they run into something interesting that they think others will find informative, they post a link and some commentary about what it is they found.

Many who enjoyed reaching the entire world with their ideas fall into this category. These people could be Web surfing for anything like new operating systems, religion reforms, computer hacks, oddball news from far corners of the world, or even the latest crochet design.

■ Second to being an actual writer is being an avid journal writer. Many blog authors started out by wanting a public journal for their thoughts. Michael, who authors Blogin Idiot, says he started a blog because he wanted the "ability to penetrate the cloud of [his] existence."

Michael did this by starting a blog journal with which he wrote deeply about himself and the things that affect him. Discovery of himself and others was his main reason for blogging.

Kat, who writes Happenstance and Geography, has a very similar take on the blog journal. When she posts about herself, she gets to know herself better, and should she be really determined but wrong about something, she says, "It takes the power of a friend's suggestion to see where [she's] faltering."

JP, mentioned earlier, also started his blog because he wanted to keep a journal and had trouble keeping one on paper. He accomplished two goals with his blog and gained a community of writer friends as well.

Starting a community blog

The only blogs that are not hinged on the development of a free-form blogging community are the blogs that are already a community. Personal blogs don't always have to be for the individual. In fact, some blogs are authored by families or by other established groups.

These community blogs have multiple authors who log in and post about what's happening, and the result is a kind of bulletin board of updates, announcements, and other communications. For family members who can never keep an up-to-date address book, these family blogs make sending holiday greetings a lot easier.

The town blog is an extremely new concept; Potrero Hill in San Francisco is one of the only communities reported to have its own blog. On this blog, local townspeople post actual local news like a recent purse-snatching or an outdoor screening of Mel Brooks's classic spoof *Spaceballs*. Its existence is brought to us through the little news blog call The Buzz produced by Blogger.com.

Branching into an audioblog

Journal blogs don't always need to be deep, unending logs about the authors' thoughts. With the invention of audioblogging by Blogger.com, an author can create a blog of audio files in place of text by calling a designated phone number and following the verbal prompts.

These audioblogs are becoming the new sensation for those people who have probably already started a normal blog but are now going on a road trip, vacation, quest, or another type of journey. Unfortunately, I have never heard of audio commenting, but that doesn't mean that these audioblogs don't get comments.

Audioblogging isn't just a special type of blog. Audio can also be used in conjuncture with any normal text blog. Audioblogging allows people to spice up their text blog with the occasional audio file.

It's a lifesaver if the author can no longer get to the Internet and type out a post. Instead, they can simply call in their post and continue to maintain the interest of their readers. This invention really plays to the need to stay connected, which, as I have said, is a core feeling for the blog author.

Addiction to photoblogging

Photoblogging has become popular with the artistic blog authors and those who just enjoy sharing pictures. Blogger.com has made this extremely easy with a new control button on the posting window or a free downloadable program called Hello created by Picasa, both of which upload the photos for free.

Like the audioblogging, the photos can be posted in between the normal text of an average blog. However, artistic blog authors can sometimes have blogs that are nothing but pictures with only a single line of text. A picture can speak a thousand words, in their opinion. Just because there often seems to be no point to the pictures doesn't mean that there are no commentators.

My favorite photo blog is *ad*RANTS, a blog covering the advertising industry. Advertising is a "natural" for the photo blog medium: if the *ad*RANTS bloggers are discussing a magazine ad, they show a color image of the ad. If they are discussing a new TV commercial, they include a color image of a frame from the commercial as well as a link where you can watch the commercial online.

To blog or not to blog?

A blog author, unless subsidized by a corporate client, is not under contract to keep his or her blog maintained—and that has led to some dead blogs out there on the Web. Unfortunately, these dead blogs are just as common as the very active ones.

People can't always stick to blogging regularly after they start a blog. Since I started blogging in November of 2004, at least a quarter of the authors in my regular network have stopped blogging. Some have burned out and left their blogs after only a few months.

Life is just not stable, and over time people can lose the time they had available for their blog. Due to time constraints, my blogging has slowed since I first started. I blog when I have time to deal with it in my schedule. The lack of activity did cost me some readers, but loyal readers stuck around.

Blogging is still considered by some to be just a new techno-fad. Since fads will come and go, people don't like to subscribe to them. My colleague JW is a prime example of this senerio.

JW has an intelligent mind, which always has something to say, but he doesn't keep a blog. His wife, an editor, keeps telling him that he should blog, especially when he's in the middle of telling me how the world works.

But JW believes blogging is not worth his precious time and that the fad will fade out with the next Web hype. Although he fits the most common description of a blog author as described by the BBC report: male, young, intelligent, professional with a degree, he prefers to leave the blogging to others.

In conclusion

Blogging has become a complex culture with multiple blog providers, blog lists, famous blog authors, and much more. If it can be done online, then it is being done on a blog some-where to some author's and reader's enjoyment.

However, these blog authors are not posting to read their own words. They are posting to understand themselves or their abilities, to connect with other people in a global blogging com-munity, and to generally explore this world through blogging.

CHAPTER 6

BLOGGING FOR
YOUR BUSINESS

Many business organizations have embraced Weblogs or "blogs" as the future in communication. In fact, a recent article in *Business Week* magazine calls blogging a "prerequisite" for business. That same article declares that blogs are "simply the most explosive outbreak in the information world since the Internet itself."

What business in the Information Age wouldn't be influenced by incorrect, stifled, or a complete lack of information? Blogs are the new conduit for business information for both internal and external use.

Blogs are available 100 percent free, not password protected, with no banners or ads. A selection of simple precreated formats and easy control programs allow anyone to start a blog with little to no technical knowledge. With such accessibility, blogs stand out as the alternative to an expensive Web site with a greater degree of marketing ability.

Business growth is a common result of blogging since blogs are a flexible, pliable form of communication that generates information in a time-line manner. Keeping to the true "blog form" is the key to gaining so much information. Blogs are successful because their basic format produces a free exchange of information between the posting parties and the commenting parties.

The exchange can seem overwhelming at first, but many find a blog much more organized than e-mail and less rigid than a newsletter or Web site. Blogs have also grown in popularity due to the large variety of uses for the Web-based media.

RULE 10:

The key to getting results from a business blog is to define the results you want to get before you start. Do you want to increase online sales by generating more traffic on your Web site? Create a favorable image for your company or product? Get your side of the story out in an honest manner to combat bad PR? Keep your employees, vendors, customers, investors, and other stakeholders up to date on company activities and plans?

Advertising, marketing, and PR blogs

Bob Cargill, of Yellowfin Direct Marketing, is an advocate of blogging for marketing professionals.[1]

Says Bob, "Most marketing and public relations professionals know a blog when they see one, but when it comes to actually using this relatively new, self-publishing platform, there are still many skeptics and naysayers among us. This time next year, however, those people will likely have come to their senses. Today I dare say you would have to be either misinformed or just plain obstinate to not at least consider adding a blog to your business plan."

Here are some reasons, according to Cargill, why marketing professionals should blog:

1. *Blogs are interactive.* In many cases, marketing is a monologue, a well-choreographed sales pitch to an audience of passive prospects. But one of the key attributes of a blog is that it allows readers to provide honest, public feedback that is posted below the author's spiel. It involves your audience. By granting the opportunity to respond almost instantly to any and all posts, a blogger is building a mutually beneficial relationship with his or her constituency. As the level of confidence grows between a blog and its readers, so does the potential for lucrative, new business activity.

2. *Blogs are humanizing.* A blog may be dependent on cold, Web-based technology for hosting and distribution, but its success depends on the ability of its author to come across as honest, credible, and down-to-earth. There is no spinning of the truth in the blogosphere. The idea is to break through the corporate-speak and to put a fresh, trustworthy face on your organization. Like a good newspaper column or editorial, most blogs are written in one strong, opinionated voice and don't shy away from controversy and difficult subjects. Some of the best business blogs in existence are some of the most candid.

3. *Blogs are inexpensive.* In most cases, the only cost to the author of a blog is the value of the time and talent required to create and maintain it. Sure, some hosting services, like Typepad, charge a modest monthly fee. But there are plenty of free, ad-supported blogging services and tools available.

Cargill's blog, A Fine Kettle of Fish (written under the aegis of Yellowfin Direct Marketing), uses perhaps the most popular one of them all, Blogger. It doesn't matter which service and tools you use to publish yours, however—the financial barriers are so few and far between, you almost can't afford *not* to establish a presence in the blogosphere.

4. *Blogs are immediate.* If timeliness is a critical element of your publishing plan, blogging is an irresistible platform. A blog makes it possible for the everyday communications professional to almost instantaneously distribute newsworthy, thematic content to a large, like-minded audience—without many, if any, layers of approval. A blog also allows you to draw out invaluable feedback without having to lollygag through the traditional rites of business courtship. Comments from readers are akin to free market research. If your goal is to establish an open, online dialogue with prospects and influential people who might otherwise not give you the time of day, a blog just may be your entrée—it certainly is a unique icebreaker.

5. *Blogs are infectious.* Like any good viral marketing campaign, the content of the best blogs is passed from reader to reader, extending the author's reach—and influence— exponentially. Bloggers are notorious for linking to other blogs that they recommend and respect. And other related sources of news, information, and opinion—even offline, traditional publications—won't hesitate to pick up an interesting post and republish it. So, in effect, a blog gives you the power of a syndicated columnist. What's more, search engines such as Google are all over blogs, especially when they're updated regularly. Blogging results in more top placements than you ever could have imagined for you and your organization.

6. *Blogs are empowering.* Today's consumers and business prospects are desensitized to the sales pitch. They've seen and heard it all. Such rampant skepticism reared its ugly head in a recent Gallup survey, which ranked people in advertising very low for their honesty and ethics. Ouch! At the very least, we may as well accept this much: we have lost more than a modicum of control.

However, because a blog is such an open, grassroots medium, unadorned and unplugged, its trust factor is high from the get-go. The format alone is engaging and empowering. With RSS, the audience decides what they want and when they want it. They have the upper hand. And by giving recipients the authority to post their own comments, it's easy for the public—and fellow bloggers—to hold advertising, marketing, and PR pros accountable for their claims. Think quid pro quo.

7. *Blogs are enjoyable.* There are many sound business reasons to blog, but let's not forget how much of a pleasure they are for both author and audience. Most blogs are quick and easy to absorb, and a refreshing change of pace from typical marketing riffs and age-old corporate-speak. Bloggers aren't just writers; they're also publishers, opinion leaders, risk takers, and entrepreneurs. They're people who are inclined to live by the mantra, carpe diem. They're passionate about their craft and evangelical about their content. And in many cases, their readers are just as fanatical.

8. *Blogs are authoritative.* We're not talking about those cathartic, diary-like blogs kept by moody, meandering teenagers. We're talking about the most sophisticated among the blogosphere, the ones owned and operated by today's savviest

businesspeople. Written by the heaviest hitters in their fields, these blogs go a long way toward formalizing their authors' knowledge, insight, and overall sphere of influence. Ideally, your blog will provide readers with plenty of fresh, premium content they can't find anywhere else. If your commentaries are consistently on the mark, your blog may soon become a frequently visited destination and raise your industry profile to unprecedented heights. But you had better think twice before posting. If you haven't done your homework, your readers won't hesitate to call you out.

9. *Blogs are valuable.* A blog is tailor-made for storing and managing your intellectual capital. It's a centralized repository for experience and expertise, an incredibly easy way to disseminate key, timely information to an audience of readers who are already interested in what you have to offer. The cost to set up and maintain a blog is practically nil. And the dividends— for those on either side of the equation—can be priceless. As Jeremy Wright, author of the business and technology blog Ensight, says: "Anything which can get the right info to the right people at the right time, empower your company to become a thought leader and let you know what your customers and the industry are thinking about you in real time is something that has massive value."

10. *Blogs are popular.* As recently as five years ago, there really weren't that many blogs in existence, but today the blogosphere is growing so rapidly that it's only a matter of time before this revolutionary, new medium reaches the tipping point. If you use press releases, newsletters, and bylined articles to promote your products and people, blogs are the next *better* thing—now. In 2004, the word *blog* topped Merriam-Webster's

list of the ten most looked-up words. And blogs received wide acclaim in the *New York Times Magazine*'s 2004 Year in Ideas issue. Blogs are here, there, and everywhere to stay.

Corporate blogging

Blogs were originally designed to publish. At the very least, a blog publishes the company's name onto the Internet. A blog can even stand in for a full-featured company Web site.

However, instead of calling up the Web site designer to add new content, the CEO or operations manager can simply address the audience of consumers or distributors himself by posting a direct message. The blog can easily take on the task of a daily or weekly newsletter to customers updating them on changes within the company, the start of new pricing, or the development of new products. This would help eliminate the incessant requests for information by e-mail or phone call. Not to mention, sharing the company's expert opinion on the future of business, economics, and life in general gives the public a sense of getting to know the company. Building a good relationship with customers is one of the keys to having a successful business.

A company blog can also act as a media resource where information for the press is published. This keeps reporters from calling every company phone line as they try to get a quotable statement. Should a rumor get started in the general media, the company blog would be a great place to confirm or debunk any allegations.

Getting information in

Instead of just informing current or potential customers, the blog could also be a great resource for gathering information from the viewing public. This depends on keeping the commenting function operational, which might require monitoring should a business be concerned about off-topic comments and the like.

However, putting that speed bump aside, blogs create great question-answer formats. This format is also a two-way street.

Instead of the corporation posting a question to the public about its product, they can address comments from the public. A corporation could quickly learn if a particular complaint is popular among customers depending on how many others respond to the same comment. This allows the engineers or the operations department to quickly focus on the serious flaws in the product or service. Once a solution has been found, the PR manager or CEO could report the progress to the public. Hugh MacLeod, authoring the blog Gapingvoid, not only manages a high-quality tailoring company in the United Kingdom but is also a self-proclaimed "blogvertising" consultant. He has gone so far as to draw a diagram about this phenomenon of corporate input and output through blogging. His post titled "The Porous Membrane: Why Corporate Blogging Works" highlights his numbered theory on how eliminating membranes between the corporation and the consumers can be done with a blog.

The budding progress report that can start over these types of blogs can give the commenting customers a sense of importance. They will start to think of the company as a friend instead of a heartless organization that only sees dollar signs. That's when the best kind of input rolls in. Testimonials can give a company a big boost in drawing in new clients. It's a known fact that people trust the opinions of other average people.

When the public is happy, they will be publishing comments that thank the company for addressing the problem, for making it easier, or for acting quickly. Don't think that people won't bother to make those statements. There are crazier ideas in this world than that of happy replies from customers who didn't have to fill out a "1 through 5" form or buy a postage stamp.

Internal information

Blogs don't have to be public for a business to make good use of them. Internal blogs are catching on in a big way. Shel Holtz, a principal of Holtz Communication, wrote on Webpronews.com that "the opportunities for blogs internally are huge, mostly (but not exclusively) as an enhancement to knowledge sharing."

Holtz says that communication over projects can be greatly improved by blogs. An internal project blog would allow people in different departments to communicate without the confusing clatter of incessant e-mails cluttering up in-boxes. *Did she get copied on that? Did he get the memo?*

These questions can easily be erased with one bulletin-board-like blog where everyone can post a memo, an update, or a question. It couldn't get any better than when the operations manager is able just to turn to that same blog and see a mock report on how everything is coming along with the project. The larger the corporation, the more this internal blog system provides a needed service for large projects.

This same idea can be used for general internal corporate communication. Company newsletters, general memos for everyone, and departmental news could be published on an internal blog that the entire workforce has access to.

Again, this eliminates the plague of e-mails that suck the life out of employees and eat up the workday. Already many CEOs and company presidents are catching on, like Intel's Paul Otellini, who believes his blog is a great vehicle for communicating with his employees. He enjoys that the commenting creates a dialog with all of the employees. Not only does he learn from them and vice versa but he can keep everyone on the same page with where the company is heading.

Executive blogging

Internal blogging is one avenue for executives who use blogs, but many are trying their hand at public blogs. In May of 2005, the BBC news network asked the question: "Can bosses blog?" Bob Lutz, vice president of General Motors; Randy Baseler, vice president of Boeing's commercial aircraft division; and Jonathan Schwartz, president of Sun Microsystems were just some of the executives mentioned in this article. With blogs normally being the medium for straight talking, the BBC wondered whether or not blogs were executive friendly. However, score one for the executives who spoke frankly, sometimes very frankly, like this post from Rich Marcello, one of Hewlett-Packard's vice presidents: "When in your life did you stop singing? When in your life did you stop dancing? When in your life did you stop being fascinated by stories, especially your own life story? And when did you stop being comfortable with the sweet territory of silence? Food for thought. Rich."

Rich is known for these off-the-cuff daydreams and deep thoughts next to posts on topics like the last business quarter, containing such technical jargon as "BCS had an excellent Q2." Being both an executive and a regular guy while posting makes him an engaging author and a great face for the company.

This isn't always a win-win situation if the executives don't tell it like it is. Bob Lutz spoke very frankly about his optimism for the new Buick Lacrosse, but not tackling the serious issue of closing factories has made him lose credibility with readers, the BBC reports. If the public doesn't believe you, then they aren't going to read you. However, even if a company is struggling, a good executive blog can help.

Jonathan Schwartz is confident that his blog has made a positive influence on himself and Sun Microsystems. In August 2004 he told *BusinessWeek* that he knew his blog was being successful when he saw comments from people with dell.com and ibm.com e-mail addresses. His salespersons also reported an increase in business from customers who viewed the company blog he authors. Though Sun Microsystems has been ailing against competitors, Schwartz remains optimistic, stating: "There's a free market of ideas out there, and I'd rather be driving the dialogue than be run over by it."

Employee blogging

An informal version of the executive blog is the employee blog. According to blogger and branding consultant Jennifer Rice, there are hundreds of Microsoft employees who maintain a blog.[2]

"Blogging is a medium, just like an e-zine or a Web site or an ad or an article," says Rice. "It's just a medium. What is done with the medium rests in the hands of the creator. The beauty of blogs is that it's a medium based on digital networking. I have a ton of inbound links to my blog, which means that I come up extremely high in Google searches."

Employees have been the ones to operate public company blogs from time to time, but most employee blogs are unofficial. Contrary to executive blogs, employee blogs have notoriously led to the author's downfall. Companies appear very concerned over what their employees might be saying on their blogs.

Russell Buckley, a leading practitioner, speaker, and commentator on mobile marketing who authors The Mobile Technology Weblog says that "if you're worried about what employees might write about you, you've got some pretty fundamental problems in the company."

However, secret company projects, mergers, and just plain griping can't be avoided sometimes and could easily be published by an employee for competitors and customers to view. Yahoo! has gone as far as to have their friendly unofficial-but-official blogger Jeremy Zawodny publish the "Yahoo! Employee Blog Guidelines: The Official Version and My Own Advice" to give them some measure of control over their employees' blogs. However, Yahoo! encourages blogging in the hopes that the blogs generated by their employees will produce more buzz over their expanding Web portal.

For those companies that aren't as Web savvy, Blogger.com has tenderly produced some general guidelines: "How Not to Get Fired Because of Your Blog." This article was created in response to the publicized firing of Michael Hanscom from Microsoft in October of 2003.

To make a long story short: Michael was working as a contract worker for Microsoft's print shop and happened upon a shipment of Apple computers being delivered to someone on the Microsoft campus. He couldn't resist snapping a shot and posting it on his blog along with the phrase: "It looks like somebody over in Microsoft land is getting some new toys."

The next Monday he was canned, and Blogger.com realized that many of its clients could fall into the same pit. The author of Blogger.com's public blog, The Buzz, is a young, excited employee by the name of Biz Stone. However, Biz's posts are strictly about Blogger.com or its many blogging clients.

"Create enforceable guidelines similar to those you've established for talking with the press, but include provisions for blogs, such as bans on off-color language," advises catalog marketing consultant Katie Muldoon in her column in *Direct*. "Explicitly tell blog users what will happen if they do not follow your regs."[3]

Muldoon also warns companies to "keep on top of what is being said" on their blogs. "Monitoring also can keep you informed about what other blog sites are saying about your company."

In an interview with *Fast Company*, blogging consultant Alex Havalais advises, "The first thing you want to do is get permission from your company, unless you choose to blog anonymously, which won't help much from the career perspective." He advises employees who blog not to write anything that they wouldn't want to see in the *New York Times*.[4]

Havalais warns that blogging has the potential to harm one's career, noting that it's pretty standard today for anyone interviewing you for a job to Google you beforehand. So you don't want inappropriate things showing up. "The most dangerous aspect of blogging is that once it's out there, it's out there [permanently]," he says.

If an employee does get into trouble for a blog, their best bet would be to read some of the labor laws that could apply to blogging. The Electronic Frontier Foundation has a thorough list on its Web site of all the laws that might protect bloggers who receive negative attention at work because of what they post on their personal blogs. Employees who blog should either blog solely about and for their company or not at all, since mixing work and personal blogging seems unadvisable.

Small-business blogging

Small and new businesses are really just tiny corporations. Corporations have all the above reasons to create a company blog, and so do the small "Mom and Pop" businesses, not to mention the self-employed. With no price tag on blogging, any starting-out business owner can create a blog and start talking about business trends or company changes instantly. A small business blog can be as diverse or as simple as the business it represents.

For a small business, blog posts become a time line to show the direction and stability of the business. This can come in handy for the owner since it can produce an annual report on how the business is growing.

An example would be if reading and commenting slowed in the third quarter, then the change that took place during that time could be affecting the success of the business. If the volume of visitors and commentators has only increased since the start of the blog, this could indicate growing visibility. The feedback could also provide a psychological boost to the struggling self-starter who is in doubt about continuing the business.

Promoting blogs

For the self-employed, the promoting blog has become a common tool. Ana Marie Cox succeeded in promoting herself with her blog, Wonkette, which got her the job of covering the National Democratic Convention for MTV. Her story of self-promotion is highlighted at Hotjobs.com as advice for the career minded.

More and more writers are promoting their manuscripts through blogging. Blogger.com has already had a few success stories, which prompted the creation of another advice article called "How to Get a Book Deal with Your Blog." In this article we learn about Wil Wheaton, who scored a three-book deal with the publishing company O'Reilly with the help of his blog. Even Blogger.com's Biz Stone has gotten a publishing deal for a book on blogging.

Profile of a business blog

Business blogs seem to possess certain characteristics in order to be successful. Blogs have grown in popularity because they are a unique form of communication. Blogs are public but not formal; they are factual and opinionated; they are never stagnant; and always passionate.

Passion makes people want to spread the word about something and inform people. A great business blog will not only be passionate about its product or service, but it will also provide relevant information on that topic.

Accountants who have their own blog have been known to provide financial calculators or links to articles that explain how to make informed financial decisions. Wouldn't it be nice if a manufacturer's blog provided a link to the scientific study backing the creation of its new product?

With passion people also become opinionated. The author of a business blog should be able to form a concrete opinion about trade developments, new products, or the economics that shape his or her business.

Relaying this information to the public helps them form an opinion about the beating heart of the business and build that all-important customer relationship. Adding a fluent, educated opinion turns the business blog into an engaging seminar instead of a flat business news report.

Complete with constant updating, passion can carry a business professional through business blogging without ever needing to read a how-to-blog-successfully article.

The add-ons

There are two common devices business professionals can add to their company blogs besides the common commenting function: a "hit counter" and an RSS system. Both these devices add to the instant sharing of information, which is the main principle of blogs.

To allow the business professional to know if his or her blog is being accessed, a hit counter can be implemented as a simple traffic analysis/statistic device. Many counter services are available on the Web and can count everything from blog visitors to how many times a particular link was accessed.

AmazingCounters.com offers these simple devices for free, with 350 different designs and Web site statistics available daily or weekly. With this information a business professional will know if people are finding the blog and accessing any information.

If one particular link is very popular, a business blog could gain more traffic if more similar links are created. A visible hit counter on the blog itself shows new guests how many others have visited this blog and gives the reader a sense of popularity.

An RSS system can enable the public to know exactly when updates are made. RSS-aware programs are now a hot item in new or updated Web browser applications and will soon be the norm.

In essence, once a change is made to your business blog, the daily, weekly, or hourly scan from an RSS-aware device or a "news aggregator" picks up the new version and brings it to the attention of the person who initiated the repeating search. This device saves time for the reader who is probably easily disappointed visiting a Web site or blog frequently and not finding anything new.

Blog vs. e-zine

Business blogs have a lot of potential. No other form of media has the same flexible structure yet unlimited applications. Besides being free and easy to manage, blogs can be used in conjuncture with any other form of communication and with any business type.

With such a variety of uses, blogs may in time become the new busy hubs of the business world. However, many business professionals will do well to focus first on Internet marketing methods that bring a more immediate and measurable return.

For instance, if you have limited time for writing, I would recommend you publish a free e-newsletter instead of a blog. (I do both.)

A number of bloggers have told me, "There's not much difference between a blog and an e-zine." I disagree. There are at least three important advantages I get with my e-zine that I don't get with my blog:

1. With my e-zine, I own all the names in my subscriber database. That list has commercial value. I can rent it, swap it, and sell other people's products to it as an affiliate. (I make thousands of extra dollars a month through such affiliate deals—with no work on my part.) With my blog, the RSS feed owns the names—I never see them.

2. With my e-zine, I can send out a message and know it will be received by my forty thousand subscribers the same day. With my blog, I have no idea how many people get it via RSS feed—or how many of those go to the new blog entry when notified.

3. With my e-zine, I can actively promote my own products and services to the list. E-zine readers accept and expect promotions. I wouldn't dare do that on my blog; it seems to violate the unwritten rule of blogging as a "pure" content medium.

If you want to market your product or service over the Internet, I strongly urge you to distribute your own e-zine free to your customers and prospects. There are several reasons for doing so.

First, the e-zine allows you to keep in touch with your best customers—indeed, with all your customers—at virtually no cost. Because it's electronic, there's no printing or postage expense.

Second, by offering potential customers a free subscription to your e-zine, you can capture their e-mail address and add them to your online database. You can then market to these prospects, also at no cost.

Whether you are generating leads or direct sales, there are two ways to sell your products and services to your e-zine subscribers. One is to place small online ads in the regular issues of your e-zine. These ads are usually a hundred words or so in length, and include a link to a page on your site where the subscriber can read about and order the product.

Or, you can send stand-alone e-mail messages to your subscribers, again promoting a specific product and with a link to your site.

When broadcasting e-mail marketing messages, your own e-zine subscriber list will get the best response and generate the most sales, far outperforming any list you can rent. "Companies are realizing that existing customers are much more responsive to e-mail marketing than customers on rented lists," says Morgan Stewart of ExactTarget. He notes that such in-house customer e-lists are growing at an annual rate of 38 percent.[5]

My monthly e-zine, *The Direct Response Letter* (go to www.bly.com to subscribe or view back issues), is not the most successful or widely read e-zine on the planet. Far from it. But marketing results and comments from subscribers tell me my simple formula for creating the e-zine—which, including copy and layout, takes me just an hour or two per issue to complete from start to finish—works. By using my simple method, you can produce an effective e-zine of your own, sitting at your computer, without hiring a writer or designer, in just a single morning or afternoon.

When you are dealing with a free e-zine (as opposed to an online newsletter that the reader pays for), people spend just a little time reading it before they delete it with a click of the mouse. Therefore, I use a quick-reading format designed to allow the subscriber to read my e-zine online right when he opens it.

In this formula, my e-zine always has between five and seven short articles. They are usually just a few paragraphs each.

Every article can be read in less than a minute, so it never takes more than seven minutes to read the whole issue, though I doubt most people do. You can see the most recent issue at www.bly.com to get a feel for the length and content of these articles.

I advise against having just a headline and a one-line description of the article, with a link to the full text of the article. All this clicking forces your subscribers to do a lot of work to read your articles, and that's not what they want.

I don't "make a production" out of it and use HTML; it's just straight text. This way it is easy and inexpensive to produce. In fact, many readers have told me they like it this way, and that they don't like HTML e-zines, which look (a) more promotional and less informational and (b) seem to have more to read.

When preparing your text e-zine for distribution, type your copy, in a single column, in Times Roman or another easy-to-read typeface.

The column width should be sixty characters, so you can set your margins at twenty and eighty. However, to make sure the lines come out evenly, you must put in a hard carriage return by hitting "enter" at the end of each line.

There are a variety of services and software programs for distributing your e-zine as well as your e-mail marketing messages to your online database.

My frequency is monthly, though occasionally I do a second issue if there is major news that month.

Let me show you specifically how having an e-zine helps bring in business for me as a freelance copywriter.

I recently gave a speech on software direct marketing. It was recorded, so I had audiocassette copies made. In my e-zine, I offered the cassette free to any subscribers involved in software marketing—potential clients for my copywriting services.

Within twenty-four hours after I distributed the e-zine, we received more than two hundred inquiries from marketing managers at software companies requesting the tape, many of whom needed copy written for direct mail and e-mail to promote their software.

By comparison, most copywriters tell me that when they send postal direct mail to a list of prospects, they average a 2 percent response. At that rate, they would have to send out ten thousand pieces of mail to generate the two hundred leads I got in an hour for free.

That's what an e-zine can do for you. Once you build your subscriber list, you have an incredibly powerful marketing tool and the most valuable asset your business can own: a database of buyers with e-mail addresses and permission to mail to them at any time.

CHAPTER 7

THE RISE OF THE
CORPORATE BLOG

Back in the days before e-mail, online e-zines, indeed, before even computers, there was the simple daily diary. Complete with lock and key, every mundane chore and bit of scandalous gossip was recorded without a thought that anyone—except the possessor of the key—would ever be privy to the thoughts and feelings expressed on the page.

We had no idea what would be coming down the pike—or over the Internet. Who knew that someday in the not-too-distant future, the in-thing of the new millennium would be the keeping of an online diary, or blog, wherein millions of ordinary folk would feel free to natter away about everything from poetry to stock futures and a myriad of other subjects?

Given the speed of the Internet and humankind's need to chatter, it wasn't long until a new twist on the personal blog appeared. The world's largest coffee klatch of conversation blew open, and corporations, taking note of the increased presence and attention being paid to political blogs, saw the chance to adapt the idea into a new marketing, staff communication, and public relations venue: that of the corporate blog.

Implemented by companies for both internal and external communication, corporate blogging via the Intranet or Internet—whether started by an executive, public relations, a marketing department, or an individual employee—can be a powerful new way to strengthen relationships with existing business partners and customers as well as attract new customers and add new suppliers.

"The corporate blog phenomenon is a grass-roots phenomenon that tries to restore the connection between companies and consumers," says blogger Steven Friedman.[1] Yet a September 2005 survey by Guidewire found that only 16 percent of companies with annual sales of $10 million or more are currently blogging.

Innovative big companies like IBM, Microsoft, Yahoo! and Google are blogging. Six of Hewlett-Packard's vice presidents maintain blogs. General Motors began Fastlane.gmblogs.com to discuss all things cars and trucks.

In an online article for *Information Week*, GM's vice chairman Bob Lutz says, "We've found the blog to be a hugely effective communications tool and a terrific way to conduct a grassroots, largely unfiltered conversation with GM fans and non-fans alike." He credits the site for its relaxed tone. "The key is to leave the corporate-speak behind and keep the tone conversational, open, and honest. Anyone who has read our blog sees the real deal, as produced by us and not polished by several layers of trained communications pros."

Lutz maintains that it is important to discuss negative as well as positive subjects, saying, "We'd take a credibility hit if we posted only rosy compliments, and credibility is the most important attribute a corporate blog can have. Once it's gone, your blog is meaningless."[2]

GM's online code of ethics states that through the blog, they promise to publish the truth; will not delete comments unless they are spam, off-topic, or defamatory; will directly link to online references and original source materials; and will disagree with opinions in a respectful way.

Visitors to Fastlane.gmblogs.com can read everything from Lutz's thoughts about his visit to a manufacturing facility in Brazil to Saturn general manager Jill Lajdziak's plans to bring back the line's name brand in a quality way.

Internally, a corporate blog can be used as a virtual meeting site where employees can communicate more compatibly, quickly, and efficiently within work groups, or, as in companies such as IBM, Microsoft, Google, and Yahoo!, individuals can maintain personal blogs. Even so, as word spreads, new corporate blogs for internal operations and external customer comments and feedback pop up every day.

The future looks bright for speaking one's mind via the written word—as long as it doesn't go against company policy or give away corporate secrets. Thanks to blogs, anyone with Internet access is able to discuss what senior executives might deem confidential information. With a click of the mouse, sensitive material could find its way into the blogosphere or onto the front page of the daily newspaper.

But companies, especially large ones, have been quick to establish clearly defined corporate rules and regulations to eliminate such situations. Yahoo's personal blog guidelines state, "Yahoo! believes in fostering a thriving online community and supports blogging as a valuable component of shared media" but cautions its bloggers that failure to abide by its guidelines in writing about Yahoo's business, products, or fel-

low Yahoos and the work they do on their own or other sites
can result in "serious ramifications" including legal action[3]

Do we need a blog?

Should every company start a blog, and, if it does, what
should be its purpose? According to a survey conducted by the
Pew Internet & American Life Project, eight million Americans
admit to having created blogs. But the question is, how many
people are reading them?[4]

A corporate survey conducted by Backbone Media, Inc., a
Boston-based Internet marketing firm, states that corporate
blogging isn't growing as fast as blogs about hotter topics such
as politics.

"We were surprised to discover that there are not as many
corporate blogs on the Internet as the volume of current
media interest might indicate," says the survey authored by
Stephen Turcotte, founder of Backbone Media, and assistants
John Cass and Kristine Munroe. "Even though a few companies have several hundred, if not thousands of blogs listed,
not every blog at a major company had a lot of posts and
comments."[5]

Although the potential for abuse exists—and some bloggers have been fired and prosecuted—there are many good
reasons for businesses to consider blogging. Word-of-mouth
praise or protests delivered by satisfied customers or
unhappy suppliers quickly deliver results. And with blogging's almost-instant ability to connect company to customer, it represents a powerful new way to communicate on
a more personal level.

Businesses start up blogs for many different reasons,

including building and maintaining relationships, improving their corporate image, and gaining valuable feedback.

Stonyfield Farms, a yogurt maker based in Londonderry, New Hampshire, started its blog to build customer loyalty and address concerns. Says its CEO Gary Hirshberg in a recent *Wall Street Journal* interview, "The blogs give us what we call a handshake with consumers, a bond of loyalty and mutual trust that's different than the typical selling relationship, where it's all about price."[6]

Stonyfield's bright, friendly Cow-munity blog explains itself as "a chance for you to look inside Stonyfield and get to know us, and us to know you." In the impersonal world of big corporations, Stonyfield's tagline alone is a strong and open invitation to log on whether you're a returning customer or a first-time visitor.[7]

Divided into four sub-blogs, customers can visit the site to discuss and share parenting issues in the Baby Babble section. Women looking for fitness advice, health tips, and stress-fighting strategies visit the Strong Women blog, a site not just dedicated to Stonyfield.

For instance, Web visitors can join a discussion about another company's controversial ad for body lotion. The Bovine Bugle introduces blog visitors to cooperative farm owners who supply ingredients to Stonyfield Farm and other tidbits that make the company seem small and personal. Blog browsers will learn that Jersey cows weigh an average of nine hundred pounds and produce an average of 4.5 gallons of extra-creamy milk with a high degree of butter fat per day.

The Creating Healthy Kids blog offers information about Stonyfield's Menu for Change program that strives to promote healthier menus in public schools and increases the company's caring-for-its-community image.

RULE 11:
Don't believe those who tell you, "Every business needs a blog." The truth is, you don't *need* a blog—and you'll do fine without one.

Setting corporate blogging goals

Today's customer is savvier than ever before. With the click of a mouse, Internet search engines can access corporate sites all around the globe.

Faced with an overwhelming number of options, a customer can locate the best deal, find the most reliable product, begin to build a long-lasting relationship with a company, register an opinion, learn new information, feel good about a purchase, or make his or her complaints known in a public forum.

It is because of this power that corporate giants and small businesses should take the time to think through a blog start-up and establish its goals. Whether you work in public relations for a Fortune 500 Company or in a small business with ten or fewer employees, you must have definite ideas about the purpose of your blog.

Is it to become an authority in your industry or on your product or service? Strengthen your company's brand or reputation? Attract new customers? Recruit new employees and post job listings? Improve customer relations by providing a place for feedback, questions, satisfaction surveys, and/or complaints?

"What we see with successful blogs is a chain reaction that starts with a sincere interest on the part of the bloggers to provide their audience with great value in terms of useful and engaging content in the form of information, help, discussion, and ideas," says the Backbone Media study. "If a company can harness their customer's knowledge and ideas, a company will find better ways to satisfy their customers' needs and wants. Listening to customers and acting on their suggestions is one of the best ways to build a group of customers who are committed to expressing their goodwill to their community."

For Microsoft marketing and finance staffing manager Heather Hamilton, her personal blog helps in recruiting efforts for the company. In a recent *Wall Street Journal* interview, Hamilton says her blog is one of about fifteen hundred written by Microsoft employees. She writes about jobs that need filling and about hiring trends. "When I started my blog, I didn't realize it would become part of my job," she says. "I wanted to help people think about Microsoft as a career destination."

Where and how to begin a blog

Companies with bigger budgets and the desire to have an interactive Internet presence can contact an agency such as Richards Interactive of Dallas, Texas, a firm that specializes in online strategy for clients as diverse as Nokia, Travelocity, and Dr Pepper/7-Up.

Their "project blog" took a network of personal sites chosen through an online demographic survey and connected clients with bloggers who were willing to try a product or service and then write about their experience on their personal sites.

But business blogs do not have to cost thousands of dollars, nor do they have to be as sophisticated as some of the ones you'll find in larger corporations. Anyone can establish a corporate blog.

The most well-known free publishing system is Blogger, a small team within Google.com, whose services include free hosting. In very little time, you can create an account, name your blog, and choose your template. Nonprofit organizations, whose budgets are always razor thin, have established blogs as an effective way of getting out breaking news and updating the organization's activities on a daily, weekly, or monthly schedule.

Making the most of your corporate blog

Although small companies and huge corporations may have different goals and objectives, all businesses that start corporate blogs want them to be successful. And while quality content and eye-catching graphics are an extremely important part of the blog, it can be the smaller things that get overlooked. When writing text for your blog, take into consideration the following details:

- Use your "voice." No one talks or writes like you do. Keep your tone conversational and easy to understand. Using a personal tone puts your readers at ease and encourages them to return each time your blog is updated. Remember that your blog—even if it is a corporate venture—is personal. Put your personality behind your words.

- If you don't feel qualified to write a blog, hire someone to do it.
- Update your blog on a regular basis. Blogs are very time sensitive—no one wants to read old news. Make sure what you have to say is timely and relevant to your audience.
- Add links to other articles and sites that can expand upon your ideas or back up your theories. Relevant information that is succinctly presented will encourage your readers to return.
- Read the comments posted to your blog entries. Because they can be considered an "online discussion," you'll find valuable information in the feedback and comments you receive from your clients, business partners, and guest bloggers.
- Track your blog postings and get to know the regulars on your site. If something is leaked or presented in an unfavorable light, you'll want to be at the ready to head off the attack.
- Reconsider keeping all your company information private. Sometimes letting a bit of the cat out of the bag piques the interest of readers who want to learn more. A click could lead to a call and . . . well, you know the rest.

Blogging's five-year plan

Online technology continues to grow faster than we can point and click. It seems as though just yesterday we were hearing television commentators giving out Web site addresses using the entire http://www address. We thought we'd never get the hang of it. And now it's old news.

In five years, many more uses for corporate blogging will have been thought up and implemented. Companies will continue to work hard to establish and hone their image, grow and promote their brands, be accessible to their customers, and protect their planning, strategy, and corporate identity—all the while people from all over the globe will be commenting, complaining, and conversing about them through blogs.

The decision to add this important tool to your company's marketing strategy or in-house communications is an important one. Blogging doesn't demand a large corporate budget or a staff filled with techno-geeks to run. It consists of everyday folks with computers on their desks who are just a mouse click away from the Send button.

Blogging is not a growth of the same Web, but an entirely new one, according to a *BusinessWeek* cover story about corporate blogging. In the article, David Sifry, entrepreneur and founder of Technorati, the blog engine search company, says, "Blogs evolve with every posting, each one tied to a moment. So if a company can track millions of blogs simultaneously, it gets a heat map of what a growing part of the world is thinking about, minute by minute. Most blogs are open to the world. As the bloggers read each other, comment, and link from one page to the next, they create a global conversation."[8]

As the popularity of corporate blogging increases and becomes a more accepted part of business practice, there is only one question remaining to be answered: is this something your company wants or needs?

BLOGS FOR PUBLISHING COMPANIES

Blogging, which in its most basic form is journaling online—but which also has ramifications much more far-reaching—gained national prominence in 2004.

If your business is a traditional publisher, you can either view blogs as competing with your product or complementary to it. I believe that the latter view can help you use blogging to improve the level of editorial quality you deliver and (although the next statement is largely unproven) possibly help you sell more subscriptions.

Let's tackle that last statement first. As of today, no business model exists for marketing paid-subscription products—magazines and newsletters—with a blog. However, one thing we know for sure is that blogging is an effective tool for increasing Web traffic.

Search engines like content, and when you blog, you're posting lots of new content to your Web site on a regular basis. Adding an active blog to your publication's Web site will almost surely boost your search-engine rankings.

Selling subscriptions in volume directly from a blog may be a way off and won't become widespread until the first smart publisher figures out how to do it, and then others will notice and copy his or her model.

But blogging has more immediate value to publishers in two areas: relationship management with subscribers and editorial.

Prior to the Internet, the only way most subscribers interacted with the publication was through the "letters to the editor." In most publications this is not an open forum; the editor controls whose letter gets published and whose is passed over.

The Internet offered subscribers other ways to get interactively involved with the publication, such as e-mails to the editor and bulletin boards on publication-specific Web sites.

The blog essentially combines letters to the editor and a bulletin board for chatting in a single electronic vehicle. Subscribers can instantly publish their opinions about the magazine (or anything else) on a blog. Once posted, these opinions can launch a threaded discussion.

For me, the real value of my blog is editorial, more specifically research for writing articles.

When I have an idea for an article, instead of writing the entire article, I write a few paragraphs—a "teaser" summarizing the key idea—and post it to my blog. If no one comments, it may indicate that my readers are not interested in this topic.

On the other hand, if I get a heavier-than-normal volume of posts in response, I know my readers are excited by the subject. And I can go ahead and produce a complete article with greater confidence that they will read it.

Even more useful, I can go back to my own blog and read the threaded discussion my text has sparked. This use of blogs as an online research tool gives an added dimension to the article, because I can incorporate comments from readers who felt passionate enough about the topic to blog, rather than my calling them up to extract a quote from them.

So, let's say you want to test the waters with a blog for your publication. Here are a few suggestions:

- Your blog should stand on its own with its own unique URL; my blog is at www.bly.com/blog. But readers should also be able to link to the blog by clicking a button on your publication's main Web site.

- Unlike articles, which are traditionally one-way paper communications (you write it, your subscribers read it), blogs are a two-way online medium, a means of starting a lively conversation about an interesting topic. I find an effective blogging technique is to make a strong statement and ask the reader for a response. (I often end my posts with the question, "What do you think?") Another blogging technique that stimulates conversation is to withhold your opinion but ask readers for theirs.

- If you are discussing an article you have already published, be sure to put a reference to the original article in your blog post. Hyperlink that reference to the actual article online.

- Put a link from your blog back to your Web site's home page, and consider having one that goes to the order page for your paid publication.

- Unlike your magazine (and like many but not all newsletters), the blog should be the work of a single author whose voice becomes familiar to the readership over time. Obvious choices include your editor-in-chief or managing editor, although a popular columnist could also be tapped to write either your main blog or a secondary blog.

■ One way to build blog readership is to arrange mutual hyperlinks with other blogs talking about your topic or reaching your audience. Don't be a snob and link only with blogs from traditional publishers. Blogging is a meritocracy, and snubbing amateur blogs, some of which can be very influential, is a mistake.

CHAPTER 8

THE BEST OF BREED:
TOPIC BLOGS

- -

While I am not a blog lover, there is one type of blog I do like: the topic blog. I don't actively seek them out often. But whenever I stumble across one during a search, it usually engages me to the point where I want to stop what I'm doing and read more than I have to.

Topic blogs are blogs that give opinion, commentary, observation, or information on a specific, usually narrowly focused topic, regardless of whether the topic has anything to do with the author's business (it may or may not). The topic blog can be written by a consultant, a small business, a corporation, or an individual. It may have a business objective (many do) or simply exist for the pleasure of the author and its readers.

What all topic blogs have in common is that their readers come to them for information, discussion, or both on a particular subject. Even if they serve a commercial purpose, the content is—or at least appears to be—relatively truthful and free of sales hype.

I like topic blogs for two reasons: First, they let you connect, in a more intimate way than books or articles, with the mind of someone who has a passion for the same subject you do. And second, they allow you to communicate with a small community of like-minded individuals who frequent the blog and comment on it.

A good example of a well-written, engaging topic blog is The Tinbasher, a blog on, of all things, sheet metal. Written by Paul Woodhouse, the blog is a mix of commentary, opinion, and education on sheet metal. Its purpose is commercial: Paul is a metal marketer. You can take a look at www.butlersheet-metal.com/tinbasherblog.

(Don't think I am an oddball to read a blog on sheet metal. I am a chemical engineer by training and studied metallurgy in college.)

The pleasure of reading a topic blog is to become engaged with the mind of an individual who shares your interest, and from whom you can possibly learn. It also provides a forum for stimulating discussions on topics you are passionate about.

The other advantage of a topic blog is that they are more focused. As a rule, the more narrowly you define your topic, the more thoroughly, authoritatively, and effectively you can write about it. By that logic, a blog on customer service is good, but if you are a concierge or hotel manager, a blog on customer service in the hotel industry will deliver more value to you.

The ability to focus a blog on a niche topic is one of the advantages blogging has over other media, in particular books. A traditional book publisher will publish a book on customer service, because the size of the market of people interested in customer service will make it more likely that they can sell the many thousands of copies needed to make publishing the book a profitable venture.

What traditional publishers can't do so well is publish topic books geared toward smaller vertical niches, like customer service for concierges. Reason: the number of concierges is relatively small, so the book will not sell enough copies to justify its publication.

On the Internet, however, it costs almost nothing to put up a blog. You can begin publishing a customer service blog for hotel professionals right away because there is no up-front investment you have to recoup. Therefore topic blogs can be extremely niched, increasing their value to their core group of readers.

From the author's point of view, he gets all of the benefits listed for his readers above, plus a few others. To begin with, a topic blog helps position the author as an expert or even a guru in the subject, whether it's Six Sigma or stress management.

Next, as the blog attracts readership, some of that readership is naturally a potential buyer for products or services the author might be selling. Also, an active blog will increase the amount of content on the author's Web site, drawing more search-engine traffic, and therefore making the author more visible and better known.

The five types of content your topic blog should have

Let's say you want to create a topic blog. Where do you get ideas for posts? What should go on a topic blog?

The information appropriate for a topic blog typically falls into one or more of the following categories:

1. *Education.* All topic blogs, to some degree, educate the

reader on the subject at hand. A good topic blog brings readers back again and again for information they perceive they are
not getting elsewhere.

2. *Resources.* Through hyperlinks and track backs, the blog
can connect the reader to other blogs, Web sites, articles, and
other resources on its topic. As those resources reciprocate, a
blogosphere is formed in which a community of people with a
common interest is interconnected on the Internet.

3. *News.* A topic blog may have links to breaking news on
a topic, original writings by the author relating to that news
story, or a combination. Most common is to have a post where
the author briefly recaps the news, with the rest of the article
expanding on the information or responding to it.

4. *Commentary.* Topic blogs give their authors a forum for
voicing their opinions and views on the topic. Some of these
topic bloggers have no other outlet for their voice, being
unable or unwilling to get articles published in mainstream
media. Others, like me, write in multiple media. In my case,
these include my content-rich Web site, blog, articles, columns,
e-newsletter, special reports, seminars, speeches, and books.

But when I write for mainstream media, the magazine or
book editor controls to some degree what I write and the opinions I express. Similarly, when I write copy for a client, the
client dictates final form and content. On my blog, though, I
can say whatever I want unfettered.

5. *Illustration.* With the ability to add images to blogs, you
can illustrate what you are talking about. The *ad*RANTS
advertising blog is based on this model. Most items discuss TV
commercials or ad campaigns, and there is almost always an

image of the ad or commercial, as well as a link to where more of it can be seen.

Finding the right voice for your topic blog

There is no absolute right and wrong on blogging style, but in twenty-five years of writing how-to material about a limited number of topics—marketing, writing, careers, e-commerce—I have formed my own opinion of what resonates with readers, based on constant feedback.

The most effective "voice" for all informative, educational, and how-to materials on a nonfiction topic, whether in a blog or a book, is to write in an informal, conversational style—in the first person, of course.

A successful author of computer books once told me, "Good how-to writing sounds like a patient, friendly teacher looking over the reader's shoulder," and I think this is good advice.

You do not want to talk down to the reader. But if it's a choice between making things simpler so you are sure everyone who reads the blog understands, or talking at a higher level because you don't want to risk offending readers by oversimplifying, I'd err on the side of being too simple.

The main difference between writing a topic blog and a book or article on that same topic is the interactive nature of the conversation. When I am writing my topic blog on marketing at www.bly.com, I can choose from a lot of marketing topics. I lean toward topics that people are likely to have a strong opinion about, and I encourage them to share it.

On the other hand, when I write a book or article, I just put in the information I think will be most useful to the reader.

I don't consider whether it's a good topic for discussion or if it prompts the reader to agree or disagree with what I write. And that's a key difference between blogs and print media: good blogging not only presents good content, but also stimulates engaging conversations through comments.

Why you don't need to be a qualified expert to start and write a topic blog

One of the reasons blogging advocates love blogging, I suspect, is that they feel it levels the playing field, allowing anyone to be published.

"Bloggers are ordinary people, many of them uneducated and with nothing interesting to say," writes Ted Rall on Yahoo! News. "They're sitting in their rec rooms, regurgitating and spinning what real journalists have dug up through hard work. They don't have sources, they don't report, and no one holds them accountable when they make mistakes or flat out lie."[1]

If I want to get an article into the *Wall Street Journal*, I have to convince the editor to publish what I write. And chances are it will never see the light of day. The *Journal* is bombarded by writers wanting to contribute material, has very strict standards, and can publish little of what is offered them.

Selling a book to a mainstream New York book publisher these days is also more difficult than when I started writing books in the early eighties. To sell your book idea to a publisher, you must write a book proposal, find an agent, get an editor interested in your book idea, convince the editor that you are an expert in your topic, and then hope the editor can convince her or his editorial board to make you an offer on the book.

The problem is, just as there are so many blogs today, there are more books published than ever. In the early 1980s, the figure commonly quoted was 50,000 books published annually. Today, that figure has tripled, to 150,000 books published annually—which works out to around 3,000 books a week, or 600 new books published every business day of the year. With so many titles published, it's increasingly difficult to convince publishers that you have either a new idea or else a fresh spin on an old topic.

But to write a blog, you need no one's permission. You don't have to establish or prove your expert credentials to anyone. You can start writing and publishing on your blog from day one. There's no law that says you have to do research or be accurate or know what you are talking about.

If you want to write a topic blog but are not an expert on that topic, consider writing a "clearinghouse blog"—a blog that serves as a central point or location on the Internet for information dissemination and discussion on that topic. In this way, you are not the expert—your readers are—but you serve as the moderator, just as the moderator of a newsgroup doesn't have to know all there is to know about a topic in order to discuss it.

On a clearinghouse blog, you might concentrate on presenting short, pithy summaries of new developments in your industries, augmented by links to the original news stories and other Web sites of interest.

Publishers of traditional paid subscription newsletters often do this: they read many sources, then condense and summarize the most important news of the month in a quick-reading eight- or twelve-page newsletter. The value to the reader is that it saves

time, eliminating the need to read dozens of periodicals and Web sites, and instead allows them to get the key news with one publication that can be read in a half hour or so.

"Many bloggers are not experts in their industry, but mere observers," says consultant Justin Hitt. "Some are decision makers, but almost all are echoing secondary sources with little unique contribution."

Great topic blogs

Travel Blogs: Traveler's Point
www.travellerspoint.com/blogs.cfm

Defined as a very strong or irresistible impulse to travel, wanderlust is part envy and part deep-down desire. If you've got that same feeling, take some time to visit the travel blogs at Traveler's Point. The blogs here are just part of the site, which *caters* to travelers—the home page argues their position as a site "nurturing traveling addictions." There's a forum to post questions, an online travel guide, travel "helpers" (people in various locations around the world to contact for assistance), and, of course, the travel blogs of literally *hundreds* of globe-trotters. Wherever you desire to go, some blogger has already been there!

If you're just *curious* about a location, or want to *live vicariously* through the writer—this is the place to be. Where have you always wanted to go? Backpacking in Central America? Hanoi? How about London or Paris? Why not? Through the blogs at Traveler's Point, it won't cost you a dime!

The J-Walk Blog: "Stuff That May or May Not Interest You"
j-walkblog.com

John Walkenbach, the self-proclaimed "blogmeister" here posts some absolutely fascinating tidbits of information, storytelling, and art. Here's a recent post:

"Contrary to popular belief, slavery didn't end with Abraham Lincoln in 1863. Experts estimate that today there are 27 million people enslaved around the world. It's happening in countries on all six inhabited continents. And yes, that includes the United States. The CIA estimates 14,500 to 17,000 victims are trafficked into the 'Land of the Free' every year."

Not all the postings are controversial, but many of them can leave you shaking your head in disbelief. Human beings are absolutely fascinating, often inspiring, and many times just downright funny—and John provides a blog with almost four hundred pages of "stuff," and most of it is interesting.

On a much lighter note, he wrote of a half-hour pillow fight in San Francisco:

"Nearly 1,000 people drawn by Internet postings and word-of-mouth converged near San Francisco's Ferry Building on Tuesday night for a half-hour outdoor pillow fight, on Tuesday, February 14, 2006.

"The underground event erupted at 6 p.m. in the center of Justin Herman Plaza with a mass rush of shrieking, laughing combatants—many of whom arrived with pillows concealed in shopping bags, backpacks and the like.

"Within minutes, pillows were arcing, feathers were flying, and by the time the Ferry Building's clock tower clanged the half-hour, the plaza and hundreds of people were covered in white down that gave the scene a wintry lustre." He concludes the post with, "Fortunately, no one was injured."

Death Ends Fun: A Voice from Bombay, India
dcubed.blogspot.com

One of the greatest adventures of the Internet is that it offers you a truly *global* outlook on life. No longer are geography or social geography just subjects for the classroom; you can read about life for people around the world, through blogging and online journaling.

This is not a blog for travelers like the first one in our foray into Weblogs. This is not the voice of a tourist, but rather a *resident*, a young Indian writer living in Bombay.

Dilip D'Souza gives the readers of his blog a wonderful window into his world, through both prose and poetry. His comments on current internal and global political controversies put a new spin on our perspective. Philip's observations on the recent cartoon-related imbroglios are wonderful, and received thirty-five comments—quite a number of people wanted to share their opinions on this controversial issue.

Some of his other postings are simple musings on the oddities of life in Bombay:

"I'm sitting in a poorly-ventilated, thus sort-of musty large room. There are probably a couple of hundred people here, and you can nearly cut the carbon dioxide with a knife. We are waiting for a film to start, a free screening of a classic, on the screen that towers in front of us.

"What I have not realized is that this is a sponsored screening (which is why it is free), and so the first thing that appears on the screen is an ad film for a large manufacturer of . . . get this, air conditioners. We are sweaty and hot and breathing stale air, and that's the prospect for the next couple of hours, and what do we see? A vapid model extolling the virtues of one model of air conditioner after another, for a good ten minutes. Not quite the way to endear us to these machines.

"But I learn something, too, in between gasping for air. Many things.

"These air conditioners are built with 'I-TREK' technology!

"These air conditioners are also built with 'Red Fin' technology!

"These air conditioners come with a backlit LCD remote controller that I can see even at night!

"These air conditioners come with hot and cold option!

"Why would I want an air conditioner with a *hot* option?

This wonderful blog makes you realize that *all* of us who live in the twenty-first century share one thing: the innate human ability to find humor and irony in life's ordinary activities!

PhysOrg.com Weblog: Science and Technology
Weblog.physorg.com

I love science; I always have. Doesn't everyone find biology, chemistry, geology, physics, technology, astronomy . . . fascinating? Well, maybe not. But for those of you who do, this is the blog for you. Not all of the postings are pleasant, but all are thought provoking. A recent one documents a newspaper article on the apocalyptic vision of life on earth a thousand years from now:

"If mankind does not put its house in order, temperatures could have risen by 15C (27F) by the year 3000 and sea levels by more than 11 meters (36ft), flooding much of London, the team from the Tyndall Centre for Climate Change Research, says in a report for the Environment Agency. Abrupt changes could make Britain much hotter, or even—such is the uncertainty of the predictions—first colder and then hotter.

"This could happen if the North Atlantic current system collapsed, denying Britain the warming effect of the Gulf Stream. Ocean surface temperatures would fall by 3C (5.4F), but as the Arctic sea ice melted, they would rise again by 8C (14.4F) in an abrupt turnabout over a period of no more than about 20 years."

It's not all like this; I certainly didn't come away from the blog disheartened or worried. This is a blog in the purist sense; a compendium of articles and links related to scientific and technological developments. If you have an interest in nanotechnology, physics, space earth sciences, or computer-related developments, this is the place for you.

David Byrne's Journal
journal.davidbyrne.com

Remember the Talking Heads of the 1970s and '80s? The subject of a major motion picture, *Stop Making Sense*, they disbanded years ago after changing the face of popular music forever.

Each of the four members has gone on to do different things musically, and that's especially true of the lead performer of the group, David Byrne. He's continued to look at the world through lenses that are anything but rose colored—his music is eclectic, powerful, and popular around the world.

David's observations, and many photographs from his travels around the globe, make up the writings in his journal. Witty, acerbic, *always* respectful of social differences, David takes us to places like Manila in the Philippines, and London, San Francisco, and Boston.

His photographs (and comments!) of bicycling in the city of Manila were wonderful. He takes his "wheels" with him wherever he goes and often rides the local bus to later enjoy scenic bicycling in some out-of-the-way spot. Ever ready with his camera, he shares his outings with his readers, as if we were close friends and family.

While in London, David wrote:

"*The Independent* weekend magazine says that after WWII a number of studies and some reports by military officers estimated that only one in four soldiers actually fired on the enemy. The others weren't as mentally and psychologically ready to kill, so they simply didn't. Very annoying for the higher-ups. The ubiquitous image of soldiers rushing into battle guns blazing simply just didn't happen.

"A man named Dave Grossman was brought in to remedy the problem. He used 'operant conditioning,' a Skinnerian psychological term mixed with simulations that were closer to the actual conditions—previously gun training mainly involved shooting at distant targets and aiming carefully."

David's trip to Manila was prompted by a musical collaboration about Imelda Marcos called *Here Lies Love*. As an anthropologist would do, he immersed himself in the culture, sights, sounds, and smells of this crowded city—and we, the readers, get to join in!

If you were a fan of the Talking Heads, or continue to follow the career of this fascinating fellow, stop by his blog. It's like sitting down with the man and sharing a cup of hot, strong espresso.

The Tinbasher

www.butlersheetmetal.com/tinbasherblog

This business blog is really a treat; originating in the UK, it's steeped in Briticisms and that dry wit we've come to love in our friends across the sea. Often somewhat off-topic, the postings from blog author Paul Woodhouse reflect life in the sheet-metal business, even down to the minutia of the workday:

"Today I'm more miffed than usual. It's a sad, sad day when one of your final tawdry pleasures to help the day mosey on just that little bit easier is pried out of your none too cold or dead hand.

"Yes, I'm talking about the ban on smoking in the workplace.

"Sheet metal workers are of the old school variety when it comes to the multitask that is smoking and working. The image of some bugger welding with a roll-up between pursed lips is quite an enduring one to me.

"At our place we have myself, Jasper, and Craig who all smoke regularly with Deborah a bit of a social smoking type and John a former smoker. In that sort of environment do you think anybody gives a brass yazoo as to the health implications of said workers?

"But that's slightly selfish.

"Jasper is an old-school shipyard type. He's the sort of sheet metal smoking fella who has a fag [cigarette] in his mouth whether it's lit or not and even if he's smoked it past the filter or not. It would be fair to say that Jasper enjoys a full fag.

"In the dim and distant past Jasper had bought himself a set of new overalls and, whilst he was welding, had docked his cigarette mid-job into the pouch pocket of his new work attire.

"After a good ten minutes welding he lifted his helmet to

168 | BLOG SCHMOG

find himself smoldering at the chest. According to John he looked as though he'd either been blasted at short range in a cartoon shotgun incident or was just starting to spontaneously combust.

"Either way, Jasper turned to John and dourly complained in his droll Scottish brogue that obviously his new overalls weren't fireproof."

Most of the writing here is colorful, anecdotal, and completely engaging.

The Tinbasher is a company blog to help customers learn more about Tinpot Alley and its sister company, Butler Sheetmetal Ltd. The Tinbasher's author, Paul Woodhouse, felt a company blog would help galvanize the two companies and help with their respective marketing strategies.

It aims to offer the reader news from the sheet-metal industry ranging from steel news to new stainless steel design concepts from a small sheet-metal firm's perspective based in the northwest of England. The author has also given those of us who are not related to the sheet-metal, industry, or even terribly interested in it, a window into life as a sheet-metal worker. He's provided tips to work with sheet metal and strategies for the care and maintenance of stainless steel, very useful information for those with lots of stainless steel cookware or sinks.

Light Made Solid:
www.glassthreshold.com/education/journal/

Stained-glass painter and restorative artist Peter Boucher provides us with an extensive archive of blog postings dating back to 2004. When you consider he posts at least once a week—sometimes two or three times a week—that's a lot of writing—and reading!

His postings include exhibits he's seen, information about stained-glass art projects, such as the McDonald Memorial Peace Windows Project, job listings for stained-glass artists, and articles related to stained glass from newspapers around the country.

A relatively current post is from the *Times-Picayune* newspaper, out of New Orleans. It describes the efforts of "the Attenhofer Stained Glass Restoration and Design Studio, run by Cindy Courage-Knezeak and her assistant Jackie Borrouso. In the aftermath of Hurricane Katrina, this shop has been dealing with an absolute avalanche of stained glass repair jobs."

Mr. Boucher provides hundreds of links to exhibition photographs, as well as links to his own stained-glass art. What a grand adventure it is to "walk through the world" alongside a man who sees light and color the way he does—and magically combines the two into wonderful works of art.

His blog is educational, inspirational, *and* an effective marketing device for his own studio. Freelance artists can take note of his rigorous blogging practice and make use of it to "get the word out" about their own art.

Church of the Customer: Creating Customer Evangelists
blogs.bnet.com/church/

This blog is for all the marketers out there. With style and grace, Ben McConnell and Jackie Huba write of consumer rituals, employee perspectives, and competition in the marketplace—lots of insight, too. Ben is a bright, articulate blogging evangelist; we were on a blogging panel together at an America Management Association seminar.

The Church of the Customer blog was nominated for *MarketingSherpa's* 2005 Readers' Choice Blog Awards as one of the top group blogs on marketing and advertising. There are postings in twenty-seven categories, from companies behaving badly to podcasting; from viral marketing to good employee relations.

Their posting for a day in early February 2006 had to do with competitors and competition:

"Your competitor is recognized as the best in your industry, with the best product *and* the best service. Your competitor has strong word of mouth and what seems to be an endless stream of evangelism.

"Just how are you supposed to compete with that?

"That's the challenged posed by Yountville, California-based French Laundry, which many people consider the best restaurant in the United States. After spending some time in Northern California last week, I had the incredible good fortune to see first-hand how French Laundry rules the high-end food chain of the restaurant business.

"French Laundry does not feed the masses. It's a single location, and you'll find it in a neighborhood of homes in a well-groomed small building that many probably mistake for a house. There's no visible sign, just a preponderance of cars parked in the street nearby. Each night, it only serves about 70–80 people, whose dining experience lasts 3–4 hours. It takes at least two months to secure a reservation.

"With multiple James Beard awards and best-of designations under his belt since opening in 1994, chef and proprietor

Thomas Keller has established an influential reputation via the evangelism of critics and customers.

"In a competitive framework, *Cyrus,* run by chef Annie Clemons, meets the high expectations set by its better-known competitor, French Laundry. Being less expensive doesn't hurt *Cyrus,* but lower price alone does not establish a leadership position. That's why *Cyrus* stands out with the Chef Phone and champagne & caviar cart. Both tactics and its point-for-point quality certainly had the locals buzzing."

Pithy advice from solid observations. I highly recommend this blog to anyone involved in customer acquisition and retention.

Vegan Lunch Box
veganlunchbox.blogspot.com

Do you know the difference between a vegetarian and a vegan? How many of you eat enough vegetables? Are you looking for ways to make changes in your own diet or the diets of your children or other loved ones?

This blog is a great place to start.

Written by a self-proclaimed vegan activist, this blog explores wonderful ways to entice children and other resistive folks into eating healthy, natural foods. She describes how she came to be what she is today in one of her posts:

"When I was in eighth grade I read the book *The Philosophy of Vegetarianism* by Daniel Dombrowski. (I didn't become a vegetarian myself until a few years later, but it, along with Animal Liberation and my mom's old copy of *Laurel's Kitchen,* set the groundwork for what came later in my life.)

"The book explains how ethical vegetarianism existed for centuries in ancient Greece: 'The belief that it is wrong to eat animals was upheld by some of the most prominent ancient philosophers: Pythagoras, Empedocles, Theophrastus, Plutarch, Plotinus, Porphyry, and perhaps even Plato.'"

A thinking woman, no doubt about it; even at a very early age!

Her recipes for vegan lunch box delights just may be exactly what you need to widen your gastronomic horizons. Jennifer offers up such treats as tempeh bacon sandwiches on whole wheat bread, vegan cranberry gel, black-eyed peas with cornbread, and a heart-shaped pizza with vegan pepperoni and cheese for her children's lunch box on Valentine's Day.

Some of my best friends are vegans, and many others are vegetarians; I've recommended this site to all who are parents— it's a gold mine of culinary ideas for *anyone* who enjoys eating.

So, that's the blogging smorgasbord for the day. A little something for everyone. Now it's your turn to go out and find a blog or two that suits your fancy. And, if there isn't one out there—why not consider creating one?

RULE 12:
For blogs centering on a specific topic or subject, the ideal author is a subject-matter expert (SME) who can write, rather than a writer who has to rely on subject-matter experts for content. Reason: the SME's more intimate knowledge allows him to comment spontaneously on the subject as the spirit moves him, which is how good blogs are written.

CHAPTER 9

How to Write, Read, Subscribe to, and Enjoy Blogs

I have a confession to make: I don't like to read blogs.

Oh, I read plenty of blogs—usually when they turn up in a Google search I am doing on a topic I am researching for one of my writing projects. What I mean to say is that I do not actively seek out blogs per se, check blogs for new posts, or comment on blogs.

Yes, I have my own blog. And I read all of the posts other people make to my blog. But I am not a regular reader of other blogs.

As I said right up front in chapter 1, there is a core constituency of blogging enthusiasts, and I do not count myself among their ranks.

These blogging enthusiasts, many of whom I encountered in the wake of my early antiblogging articles, like and gravitate toward blogs for many of the very same reasons that I stay away from them.

Chief among these is the lack of editing. Says Eric: "I do read books, periodicals, and Web sites. I just add blogs to the list as another source. It's also nice to read material that is relatively unedited. It gives you a quicker insight into a person's thought processes or personality to read text that hasn't gone through the PR-speak—unsanitized reading material."

When I asked the question on my blog, "Why do you read blogs?" marketing consultant Jim Logan explained that blogs can give you a deeper connection with the author than other types of writing.

"I own a few of the books you've written," Logan said. "I like them. One in particular has helped me in my career. I thought of writing you in thanks, but never did. I always thought you were too busy or must be receiving unsolicited input all the time. In short, I always thought I'd be a bother.

"Then you started to blog and as such, I had an easy means to reach you. You opened a dialogue and I can communicate with you as easy as leaving this comment. Since then, you've e-mailed me a few times in acknowledgment of comments on your blog. We even had a short conversation on the phone. All because you blog.

"Why visit your blog? You are very good at offering insight and opinion—opening a conversation. Books, magazines, newsletters, and such are often better thought out, more informative, and better written than blogs I read . . . but I never 'met' you until you blogged.

"You're better here than in your books. You're human, one of 'us.' You lead and participate in the conversation. That's why I read and comment on your blog."

One of the best ways to learn how to blog is to read other blogs. That's not to say that others who blog are always geniuses, but you should learn a little about who is out there in your industry, how they blog, and what the "accepted norms" seem to be.

Most of you reading this book are not old enough to remember telephone party lines, but I am. And they were the telecom equivalent to today's blogs.

Unlike today, where every house in your neighborhood has its own phone line, when I was a kid growing up in the 1950s and '60s, we shared a party line with several of our neighbors.

That meant if you wanted to make a phone call, you had to wait until all of your neighbors were off the phone and the line was free.

At first, we kids loved the party lines, because if you picked up the phone receiver quietly, you could listen in on other people's calls, just as blogs allow you to read public conversations online.

You'd think that would be exciting, and it was—for about two minutes. Then you quickly realized that most conversation is blather and not worth listening to. I think that also holds true today on the Internet. Like party-line conversations, most blogs (not all, of course) are conversational blather just not worth listening to.

Using Bloglines to find blogs you want to read

Bloglines is one of the most comprehensive, integrated services for searching, subscribing, publishing, and sharing news feeds, blogs, and rich Web content. It's free and easy to use. Bloglines was purchased some time ago by longtime Internet player AskJeeves. You can sign up for a free account at www.bloglines.com.

Bloglines will become a very useful tool for you in many

ways, but for now, focus on two things. First, bloglines is a search engine for blogs. At the home page, you can type in a word or phrase related to your subject or industry and see results of other blogs that deal with that subject.

Under each blog that shows up, you will have a chance to preview the site, see other related sites, and subscribe to the site. This leads us to the second thing that Bloglines does: when you preview a site, Bloglines tells you how many people subscribe to that site. That number may indicate that a site is well established and has lots of readers.

Since this step asks you to subscribe and begin reading a number of blogs, all you need to do is find the blogs you want to subscribe to. You can find them here or anywhere on the Web. You can then come back to Bloglines and subscribe to them. You will see a link called "My Feeds." When you click on "My Feeds," you will be presented with a list of all of the blogs you subscribe to.

Become an RSS user

You may be noticing more and more little orange RSS icons on Web sites and most blogs.

As we've already discussed, RSS variously stands for Really Simple Syndication or Rich Site Summary. The former is the more commonly accepted phrase. It also helps to explain what RSS is.

RSS is a new way to both distribute and receive content online without using e-mail. Publishers use RSS to distribute a "news feed" to readers. Readers subscribe to an RSS feed via a newsreader or news aggregator. RSS is based on XML, a standard for exchanging information between Internet applications.

A newsreader is a little piece of software (it can also be an online service) that is downloaded to your desktop. It delivers a headline, a short summary, and a link back to the full text every time an RSS news feed is updated.

News sites such as Yahoo! and CNET have been publishing RSS feeds for quite a while. More recently, RSS buzz is about blogs.

Most blogging software automatically includes an RSS feed. If you subscribe to a blog via RSS, you are alerted every time the blog is updated. You can also "subscribe" to a blog via a BlogLet.com e-mail subscription if that feature has been added to the blog.

The beauty of the RSS format is that no e-mail is involved as the delivery mechanism, so there are no overflowing in-boxes or spam filters to block your e-newsletter if you're a publisher.

The downside for publishers, however, is that you don't know much if anything about subscribers to your news feed or blog. Your readers don't need to give you an e-mail address in order to subscribe. That's a plus, of course, for readers concerned about privacy.

Publishers can be sure that their blog or news updates are being successfully "pushed" to interested subscribers without being siphoned off into e-mail junk folders.

"Blogs are not sales copy," says David St. Lawrence, author of the business blog Ripples. "The few blogs that attempt to pitch rather than begin a conversation are quickly tuned out. Those that have something to say attract interest, comment, and referrals."

Bottom line: we're still in the early adopter phase when it comes to syndicating content via RSS. But it's catching on faster and faster, just as blogs are becoming more and more accepted as an online communications tool.

How to write a post on your blog

1. *Pick topics that interest you.* "Your blog is your bully pulpit," says blogger David St. Lawrence. "You get to choose the topics."[1]

Your blog is a forum to express your opinions on these topics. "Every person publishing a blog with any level of readership takes a stance on the issues, whether political, social, religious, or business," says Internet marketing expert Jim Edwards.[2]

2. *Pick topics that interest your readers.* Does this contradict number one above? Not at all. David explains, "I have topics that I write less about now because readers have indicated that they want to hear about something else. My testing happens on a weekly basis. It keeps me from wandering off on arcane tangents where I could end up writing for myself alone."

3. *Stick with one key topic per post.* If you are tempted to go into another topic, even related, don't. Instead, expand the thought into a separate entry and make it your next post.

4. *Be brief.* Don't ramble. Say what you have to say in the fewest possible words. Make your point, then stop.

If you write long essays instead of short, snappy posts, not only will people not read them, but you'll be wasting far too much of your time writing them.

"One of the things I work on with my blog coaching clients is how to minimize the time they spend writing their blog, while maximizing the ROI they'll get from it," says blogging consultant Deb Weil. "And yes, the ROI will be branding, media exposure, lead generation . . . not direct sales. One of my clients would like to get a book contract out of his blog—a reasonable goal, I think."[3]

5. *Give sources and citations for facts.* For instance, if you are talking about something Cisco did that you read about in *InformationWeek*, cite the publication, issue date, and page.

Some bloggers put a hyperlink from every source to the original article, but I don't hyperlink to the original article unless I feel the reader would benefit from reading it. If I am just repeating one fact from the article, there's no need for the reader to see it.

I think the practice of hyperlinking everything to everything else on the Internet is overdone and overrated. When you read a book, do you feel compelled to read every other book, article, Web site, and resource the author reviewed while researching his book?

Of course not. One of the ways authors add value to content is to condense, compress, and simplify, to save the reader the time and trouble of plowing through mounds of original source material. The unchecked hyperlinking of every other word on your blog to an article or Web site defeats this purpose, distracts the reader, and makes for cumbersome, slow reading.

6. *Don't rant and rave.* You may be emotional about a topic, but build your case with logic. State the facts. If you don't know the facts, consider delaying the post until you can research them. If you don't know what you are talking about, astute readers will detect this, and your blog will quickly lose credibility.

7. *Resist ad hominem arguments and insults.* Even though it is fashionable in some circles of the blogosphere to do so, don't trash other bloggers to bolster your own viewpoint.

Avoid ad hominem arguments. When you disagree with what someone else wrote on their blog, back your opinion with evidence. Do not impugn someone's character because you disagree with her writing: the person and the writing are not one and the same.

Attack the writing, not the writer. Remember, just because someone disagrees with you does not make him or her a moron or an evil person, or call their upbringing or lineage into question.

8. *Write as the spirit moves you.* Do not force yourself into a rigid schedule. Spontaneity and impulse are part of blogging's charm and style.

How to write an effective comment on someone else's blog

1. *Read the original post carefully.* Then read it again. Sometimes an emotional reaction causes us to be careless and miss part of the writer's point. We then end up criticizing something that isn't really there and making ourselves look silly.

2. *Keep your comment brief.* People read through the comments attached to a post rather quickly. If yours is much longer than the other comments, they'll skip it.

3. *Think about whether you want your comment recorded for all posterity.* Remember, once you submit a comment to a blog, it's there forever. You can't erase it.

4. *You don't always have something to say in return.* You shouldn't feel compelled to comment in response to every post made on your favorite blogs. Sometimes silence is golden.

5. *Be ready to back up what you say.* When refuting an opinion or claim, back up your argument with facts, and cite your sources, with hyperlinks to them if appropriate.

6. *Know when to stop a threaded discussion.* Of course you

can theoretically go on forever. But someone has to have the last word, and it doesn't have to be you. Go on to more productive tasks. Don't argue with everything everyone has to say all the time.

Controlling blog addiction

I've noticed that there are a number of bloggers who spend an inordinate amount of time going to blogs, reading blogs, and having protracted discussions on blogs by placing comments in response to posts and then more comments in response to comments on their original comment.

When I opined that spending all of this time on blogs was a waste of time and suggested that bloggers had nothing better to do but that other people did, one of the active marketing bloggers at the time criticized me for it. "You are not busier than me," he said. "We both have a certain limited amount of time for reading. You choose to spend it reading magazines, newsletters, and newspapers. I spend it reading blogs."

But it's more than that. My sense is that bloggers are addicted to the interactive conversation of a blog, much in the same way that people are addicted to forums and chat rooms—or, as a kid, I listened in on party lines.

I'm willing to wager that more people than would care to admit it are addicted to something. But whether it's just surfing Web sites, reading blogs, or hanging out in chat rooms, the Internet is particularly addictive.

The problem as I see it is that all these online activities take time away from more important tasks. Yes, it's fun to read a blog, to be involved in a conversation, and to see what other people are thinking.

But you can find out what other people are thinking in a variety of less time-consuming and, I think, more accurate and representative ways. In business, you can quickly find out what the key issues in a given sector are by reading the letters to the editor in that industry's leading trade publications. For the consumer market, a lot can be gleaned through observation (watching people).

When you read a letter to the editor in a trade journal, you don't spend your time arguing back and forth with its writer. But on a blog, that's precisely what you do. It may be fun, but it is not very productive.

Most people are busy today, and time is a limited resource. I would be surprised to hear that you cannot find a better, more efficient way to use your time than having animated discussions on blogs.

Promoting your blog

The question is: do you really want to promote your blog? What do you gain from doing so?

The end result of a successful Internet promotion is that it drives an increased volume of traffic to a specific URL. Should that URL be your blog? I think not.

Why not? Because when people read your blog, you don't capture their names and e-mail addresses. So you don't gain the ability to communicate with them at will. On a blog, they only hear from you if they subscribe to it on an RSS feed or visit the blog frequently.

If you do Internet marketing, my advice is to drive the traffic to the sign-up page for an e-newsletter that you write, publish, and distribute at no charge on a regular basis. To get the e-newsletter, the visitor must submit to you his name and e-mail address.

When that happens, your subscriber list becomes a valuable, easily monetized asset—a house e-mail list of prospects interested in you and what you are selling. You can place online classified ads for your products in your e-zine.

You can also send solo promotional e-zines to your subscribers between regular issues. Since they have opted to receive e-mail from you, it is not spam.

What will those small ads and e-mail marketing messages do? Generate leads or orders. If you are an Internet-marketing entrepreneur, monetizing your e-list in this way will generate between a dime and a dollar or more per subscriber name per month in gross revenues.

If I didn't have a free e-newsletter, I'd consider putting up a sign-up page at a distinct URL and driving traffic toward that. On the sign-up page, you offer some free content, typically a downloadable PDF, in exchange for the visitors' names and e-mail addresses. If you also want to capture a physical mailing address, offer them something that has to be mailed, such as a CD.

If you have no e-newsletter or content offer, then use your Internet marketing to drive traffic to your main Web site. That way, you are promoting your company and your products, and may generate interest or sales.

All of these options, in my opinion, are more productive and profitable than using Internet marketing to drive the traffic specifically to a blog.

I understand that if you have a blog, you want people to read it. But is it really worth spending time and money to build that blog readership? If your blog is not clearly monetized, then probably not—and your marketing dollars would generate a better return on investment elsewhere.

Advice for budding bloggers

Marketing expert Shel Horowitz offers the following tips for newbie bloggers:

- If you've got new content at least once a week, that should be okay.
- Know your objectives and keep the content focused on them—it's a business growth tool; no one cares what you had for breakfast.
- Blog about things that interest you but also have implications for your key audience.
- Promote your blog. "Mine is in my e-mail sig," says Shel. "I've also sometimes commented on issues that arise in various online discussion groups, and then written a response suggesting people visit. Once I sent a magazine editor there."
- Keep a file with your blog entries. "In my case, I'm putting up a kind of reverse mirror page on my own Web site, which will have my blog entries from oldest to newest, and a hyperlinked table of contents so people can find any article easily," says Shel. "This way, I'm protected if for some reason Blogger goes down or changes its service to make it undesirable, or starts rolling old posts out of the archives. I will probably mine my blog for future books and articles, just as I've done with my various e-zines."

- Very important: Before you hit "Post," copy your text into a program with a spell-checker, correct the typos, and read through one more time.

RULE 13:
Grammar, spelling, punctuation, and the other rules of written communication apply to blogs just as they do everywhere else. The reader who spots typos and misspellings will not think you are casual or relaxed about matters of grammar and proofreading; he will think you are a sloppy and careless writer—and by extension, a sloppy, careless thinker—not the impression you want to convey.

CHAPTER 10

Does Blogging
Have a Future?

What is the future of blogging? Is it already a fading fad? Or is it a marketing and communications revolution? More correctly, I think, it is somewhere in between.

If you were to ask me, "On a scale of 1 to 10, how much has the Internet revolutionized marketing?" I would answer 10 without hesitation. But when measuring how much blogging has revolutionized marketing on a scale of 1 through 10, I would say 4 when in a positive mood, and maybe 2 when I am more cynical.

Plenty of people tell stories of blogging successes. But as numerous as they are, they are isolated incidents. Companies have built successful business models for e-commerce focused on Web sites, e-zines, and e-mail marketing, but not on blogging. They may have a blog as a part of their overall Internet-marketing program, but it is not the central part.

Are blogs effective marketing tools on a widespread basis? Not according to *MarketingSherpa*. "Call us cynics," says an article in *Sherpa*. "Blogs may be hip and trendy, but they don't do diddly-squat for most people's businesses."

The proof? After four years of research, *MarketingSherpa* estimates that only 0.03 percent of the 34.5 million existing blogs are driving sales or prospective customers to their bloggers.

So after my year or so in the blogosphere, have I changed my mind about blogging? Do I now agree that blogging is a marketing revolution, and that—as Robert Scoble states in his book *The Red Couch*— "every business needs a blog"?

No. Instead, I have quite a different opinion. Here's what I've discovered:

- Blogging as a marketing tool is vastly overhyped by blogging consultants, authors, speakers, advocates, and evangelists.
- This group of hardcore bloggers has lost all objectivity concerning blogging as a medium and marketing tool.
- Blogging is, at best, a mildly effective marketing tool, and creating a blog for most businesses is strictly optional. No business "needs" a blog. Most businesses probably shouldn't waste time and resources creating one.
- Although blogs can incrementally increase sales of products and services, their ability to generate online revenue is insignificant when compared with proven online direct response marketing methods such as e-zines and e-mails.

However, blogging does have some value as a marketing medium in two respects. First, blogs can in many instances significantly improve a site's ranking in the search engine, thereby driving more traffic to that site. Second, blogs can be effective as part of an integrated program to establish one's reputation as an expert in a particular field. Therefore, blogs can help consultants and other businesses that sell expertise (either as a stand-alone service or in support of a product) increase visibility and credibility among the target audience.

Recommendation: if you want to explore blogs as a marketing tool, go ahead. A blog is ridiculously easy and inexpensive to implement.

To some businesses, driving traffic through search engines is an incidental and unimportant activity: these search-generated leads are too unqualified to be useful to them. But to other businesses, search traffic is vital to their online marketing success: if they can drive traffic to a specific URL, they can reliably and profitably convert a certain percentage of that to sales. For companies focusing on optimizing search rankings, blogging is a valuable adjunct to other search-engine optimization techniques.

The death of branding on the Internet

Many blogging consultants who hype blogs credit them as being powerful adjuncts to a company's efforts to build its brand on the Internet.

But as marketing shifts away from branding and toward ROI accountability, direct marketing plays more of a role, and the importance—or rather the effectiveness—of branding fades.

Now, I know a lot of the brightest marketing minds in the world, and Don Libey is certainly one of the top five, in my humble opinion. So, not being a big branding guy myself, I enjoyed the latest issue of Don's *Secrets of the Catalog Master* bulletin, published by list broker Merit Direct. In it, he basically says that branding is dead or dying on the Internet, being replaced by (what else?) ROI-producing direct marketing driven by Google.

Don says, "Buying is no longer a matter of who [the brand or reputation of the seller]. Shopping is a matter of word description. In other words, I will no longer associate buying pears with Harry & David.

"Instead, I will associate buying pears with the words 'pear' or 'fruit' or 'gourmet pears' or any of 58 other words or word combinations."

Don also credits eBay with diminishing the importance of online merchant reputation—as millions of people are sending money to other people they've never heard of and have no reason to trust simply because these sellers have a five-star rating on eBay.

Don calls this kind of buying "thought-activated word shopping" and says it is replacing branding in importance for consumers.

Branding may be diminishing in importance in offline marketing, too. It's not that branding doesn't matter. It's that other things, whether price or product advantages, matter more.

Top direct-response copywriter Richard Armstrong notes that "branding is just one of many credibility factors that go into an advertisement . . . you can't build your whole marketing campaign around it.

"I've always said that you could fire a high-powered rifle down the middle of Madison Avenue at high-noon on a weekday and not be in danger of hitting anyone who'd ever read a single book about advertising," says Richard.

"There is just very little in the way of what I'd call 'technical expertise' in the world of general advertising. But because it's impossible to survive in business on bull alone, a lot of these guys have focused on 'branding' as the alpha and omega of marketing.

"Get three Madison Avenue types in a room and it's 'branding' this and 'branding' that. But it's ridiculous.

"Look, I believe in branding. I'm sure you do, too. But to me, it's just one of many credibility factors that go into an advertisement.

"If the product comes from a company that people know and trust, great—go ahead and make use of that in your ad. But you can't build your whole marketing campaign around it."

Richard continues: "The fact is that 'brand loyalty,' which is the Holy Grail of Madison Avenue, is really a mile wide and an inch deep for most customers.

"I have brands that I prefer among just about everything I buy . . . but virtually every single one of them is negotiable. Show me that your product is cheaper and/or better than my current brand, and I'll switch in a heartbeat.

"I'm a big fan of Allen-Edmonds shoes, for example. For years, I was always telling people about how comfortable and well made they are.

"A few weeks ago, I was telling this to a friend of mine, and he said, 'You should try Cole-Hahn, they're better.' I said, 'No way!' He said, 'Try them.'

"So I tried them. Guess what? I now wear Cole-Hahn shoes. So much for brand loyalty!"

The conclusion: branding is just one of *many* credibility factors in marketing, and credibility is just one of multiple factors in selling, so to devote your advertising to building the brand is to do something like one-tenth of the selling job it should be doing.

Brand loyalty is fleeting. Unless your advertising provides a compelling reason why the consumer should buy your product instead of competing products, you won't be able to pull consumers away from those competitors.

Marketing consultant Jim Logan comments:

Take the Super Bowl. Days after the Super Bowl, what ads, products, and companies do you remember? Millions of dollars were spent on advertising, what do you remember?

If you're like most people, you remember a commercial or two, have a vague recollection of the companies that bought ads, but overall have little idea of the who, what, and why of Super Bowl commercials. It's to be expected.

Most commercials offer little to remember. Some are cute; I especially like the beer commercials. But I don't think any are effective at growing market share or enticing us to try a product.

None of the commercials make an offer or ask us to do anything. Most of the commercials don't seem to have a point at all, just cute video that could be used with a number of products and companies. Blah.

I'm sure there are studies that show the Super Bowl commercial-type branding works. But with who [sic]? If you don't drink Bud Lite today, are the commercials about horses playing in an open field going to make you drink it tomorrow? I think not.

I wonder what would happen if more commercials were

about the benefits of the product, the difference offered as compared to other products and services, and the reasons you and I can believe the benefits and difference is real.

The future of RSS

What about subscribing to content through Really Simple Syndication (RSS) instead of subscribing to e-newsletters and registering on Web sites, both of which give marketers your e-mail address along with permission for them to send an endless stream of promotional e-mails to it?[1]

RSS is swiftly becoming mainstream, while just a year ago it was the province of the tech savvy.

RSS provides a versatile, structured format to rapidly aggregate, distribute, and manage information. For example, RSS provides the infrastructure to distribute information on audio (podcasts) and video (vblogs or vlogs) programs. An article in *BusinessWeek* notes that "video blogs are proliferating," and that applications could include online video distribution, ad sales, and corporate sites for customers and suppliers.

As new applications develop and RSS software is made more user friendly, RSS will become increasingly invisible to the user, and discussions on its adoption rate will focus on the size of the market of users rather than on the proliferation.

Confusing and conflicting statistics appeared almost daily last year detailing the proliferation of RSS. A Forrester Research study said that just 2 percent of online U.S. households use RSS, while JupiterResearch and Pew reported adoption rates around 12 percent and 9 percent respectively.

A study from Yahoo! and Ipsos Insight found that 31 percent of online users use RSS, but most of them are unaware of its nomenclature. This is because they use it as part of other services, such as My Yahoo! and My MSN, where it is not necessary to understand RSS technology to use it.

The discrepancy in reports of adoption may result from how questions were worded in the different surveys. The Yahoo! estimates probably offer the most complete picture available at this time, because they square with the massive growth rates in RSS traffic reported by some content providers.

No longer will users need to learn the arcane of RSS when Microsoft introduces its next edition of Internet Explorer, already named Vista and scheduled for release in the near future. If the planned integration and release occur as promised, subscribing to RSS feeds will become as easy and accepted as bookmarks are today.

RSS is device agnostic. In the future, users will employ it seamlessly on multiple devices. It's already possible to receive feeds on mobile devices like cell phones and PDAs as well as through instant messaging.

With Internet users becoming accustomed to receiving and managing information as RSS feeds on their computers, they will want and expect to be able to receive them on their mobile devices. This will create opportunities for those who develop marketing, entertainment, and work-productivity applications for mobile devices.

As more Web users turn to RSS readers on multiple devices, sites providing content will see the readership of their feeds grow. The pervasive use of RSS readers, however, may cannibalize the advertising circulation of some sites.

The shift from reading content on the site to reading it in

a feed will mirror what has occurred in print newspapers, where readers are turning to online sources in such numbers that newspapers report circulation declines.

Because RSS and Web sites are both online, the circulation shifts will be subtler. But the shifts are likely. It will be important to monitor the effect of feeds on circulation. Nevertheless, there is countervailing force.

RSS aggregators/readers present a steady diet of new information in a readily digestible form, so we can expect RSS to let users increase their overall consumption of information. For marketers, this shift in consumer behavior will increase opportunities to present their messages.

However, because users can unsubscribe with a single click, marketers will have to provide value to sustain readership. The challenge will be to determine how to create and deliver a message the consumer really wants.

The arguments are compelling for the monetization of content through advertising in RSS feeds. For many content providers, monetization is essential to their business model. For the advertiser, RSS feeds offer highly targeted audiences. However, marketers trying RSS advertising will need to monitor user behavior, for this will temper how the medium develops.

Too many ads in the feed may repel readers. Once a reader subscribes to a feed, the reader no longer is compelled to visit the site to read its content. To drive the reader to the site, many content providers offer only a portion of the content in the feed. Here is a caution.

Content presented in a partial feed must be compelling

enough for the reader to want to read the full text. Unless this challenge is met, content providers can expect a reduction in click-throughs and of the views of any advertising appearing on the site itself.

These feeds are just starting to become available, and they will give users and advertisers greater control over their information in the future. However, marketers placing ads in these feeds must combine carefully selected targets and relevant ad content to drive response.

Marketers expect to measure the performance of their ad spending, and RSS is no exception. RSS performance measurement is evolving.

Current metrics are similar to e-mail, but the performance of RSS feeds differs. We should see growth in our understanding of how to measure performance and in the tools for measuring marketing performance of both RSS feeds and any ads carried in them.

Though RSS was once hailed as the solution to sidestep spam, one thing is certain: it won't replace e-mail in the near term. E-mail is entrenched as a primary Web activity. RSS presents another medium for marketers to communicate with their audiences.

RULE 14:
Blogging is just one more method of communicating online. And it is one of the minor methods, not—like Web sites, e-newsletters, and e-mail marketing—one of the "killer apps" of Internet marketing.

Coming full circle

It always surprises me how many marketing people jump on trends and become "instant evangelists" for the new thing, whether it's blogging, podcasting, or SEO copywriting—mainly, it seems, because it *is* new.

They so badly want to believe that their beloved gimmick is the "holy grail" of marketing—the silver bullet—despite the fact that such has never been found and, I am convinced, never will be.

I'm of a different school—the "show me" school. And in marketing, that means showing me that a new tool or trendy technique has a proven track record of generating a positive ROI.

Until that happens for a new marketing technique—whether it's blogging or whatever—I can't see getting excited about it. Why would you or anyone?

It does seem to me that the people who are quick to embrace the "next big thing"—even though it's far from certain to be so—are mainly the consultants who want to peddle advice on that marketing method to unwary clients.

The sad fact is that consultants and ad agencies are spending the client's money, not their own money. So of course they are fans of creativity and experimentation: it's fun and exciting, and if it doesn't work, then they still get paid. But the clients lose big time when it produces zilch in results.

In the introduction to this book, I posed a number of questions that I intended to explore during my year on the blogosphere. To sum up my blogging ideas and recommendations, here's that list once again, this time with my answers, opinions, and conclusions:

Is blogging a new and important channel for publishing and communication? Or are blogs merely an outlet for frustrated writers to post their rejected ramblings online?

Blogging is a new *alternative* channel for publishing and communication. It is the cheapest and easiest means of self-publishing yet created.

While it's relatively new, I wouldn't say it's important, or at least not more important than other media. The members of the blogosphere do not, as of yet, wield a communal power that gives them control over elections or markets.

Will blogging grow in importance over time? That remains to be seen. My opinion is that there is too much content and too many media already competing for the consumer's attention. Blogs are not powerful enough to stand out from the clutter. With so many thousands of blogs already cluttering the Internet, it's not likely that many will break through all that news in a big way anytime soon. But it is possible and does happen occasionally; look at what Matt Drudge did on the Web, or the dissatisfied Dell customer whose complaining took the form of a blog that gained national media coverage.

And yes, many blogs serve as an outlet for frustrated writers to post their rambling on the Web. The majority of what I read on blogs is simply not valuable enough, not well researched enough, or does not have enough of a hook for the author to sell it for money to mainstream publishers.

"Much of the blogging phenomenon is purely self-indulgent, puerile share-my-life-with-friends drivel," says Chris Williams. "But there are blogs in many fields—business, marketing, industrial news, and more—that offer up-to-date information, mostly in article format, for everyone to read. I regularly read the blogs of copywriters, marketing professionals, a CEO, and a professional speaker. All are 90 percent solid, beneficial information.

"Yes, I've seen many blogs that are the effective online equivalent of a high school hallway. The communication standards in many nations are slipping, and it's reflected in these blogs. But to outright dismiss the entire phenomenon is doing the good quality blogs a disservice."

Are blogs encouraging a broader audience to read and write? Or are they another vanity press publishing banal trash that "real" publishers would never even take a second glance at?

I think the Internet has turned us into a nation of writers and, overall, improved the writing skills of Americans, particular white-collar executives working in corporations.

"Resources for the express of informality in writing have hugely increased—something not seen in English since the Middle Ages," says David Crystal, a linguistics professor at the University of Wales, who contends that the Internet is getting more people to write and that this is a good thing.[1a]

But the Internet medium that made this new literacy happen is e-mail, not blogging.

When I joined the corporate world in the late 1970s, there were no computers yet, only typewriters. And in those days, no self-respecting male employee had a typewriter on his desk, with the exception of newspaper reporters.

Since executives didn't have typewriters, they dictated letters to secretaries. The secretary was the bottleneck to getting the communication out. Writing a letter was no small project;

the turnaround time was often a day or more. So people communicated mainly by phone, not in writing.

With the advent of e-mail, typewriters were replaced by computers, the post office was replaced by the Internet, and the turnaround time from composing your message to getting it to the recipient went from days or hours to literally seconds. Because e-mail is so convenient and easy, it has become the dominant form of communication in the business world— and because e-mails must be written and executives have keyboards, all businesspeople routinely write and type letters.

I'm not sure whether personal blogs are actually encouraging more people to write; people who feel compelled to put their thoughts in writing have always done so, regardless of the technology or whether they could be published. The only thing the blog is doing is making it easy to get your writing published, albeit in a nonpaid, amateur forum.

Advocates of recreational blogging praise "Citizen's Publishing" for bringing the opportunity to be published to the masses. They see it as bypassing the (in their view) exclusive, snobby world of traditional publishing that keeps many out and only a few in.

The traditional model of publishing is far from perfect, but one advantage it does have that blogging lacks is a screening mechanism. In publishing, there is at least someone in charge; in the blogosphere, no one is in charge, and at times, the inmates rule the asylum.

In what ways have blogging and the Internet changed the face of writing, publishing, PR, news, journalism, and the writing profession?

There are political and news blogs that seem to be more widely read or influential than the average personal or business blog. Politicians, corporations, and others who care how they are treated by the press monitor these blogs just as they do newspapers and TV.

Therefore, blogs can be said to have entered the mainstream of news and journalism. And because of their visibility, they will be increasingly accepted as legitimate press by the public, if not by mainstream journalists, who are usually quick to point out that blogs aren't fact-checked and bloggers aren't held to the same standards as newspaper reporters.

With the Internet "anyone could publish their work and have it sent around the globe in seconds," says John Colanzi, an Internet marketer. "Writers could bypass the traditional publishing industry and save time in getting their work to the public. They no longer had to fear that dreaded rejection slip. They could succeed or fail on their own merit." Colanzi calls the Internet "a writer's paradise."[2]

Blogging has certainly been a boon to many writers. A number of fiction and nonfiction writers have gotten book deals because of their blogs. Other writers have used blogs to promote their writing projects. "Imagine the possibilities," says Colanzi. "You can now become part of a targeted network of like-minded blogs and have your content spread throughout the entire network in the twinkling of an eye."

However, I get the sense that the Internet overall has devalued writing. When you start calling writing "content," you are commoditizing it, and being viewed as a commodity puts the seller—in this case, the writer—at a disadvantage, because commodity products command lower prices.

Writer Harlan Ellison comments: "That's part of the problem for writers, for establishing a career. Cultural amnesia due to television and the Internet. But, to answer your question directly, in terms of money, condition of work, and approbation, life is a lot harder for writers now."

I asked Ellison if he blamed the Internet. "Oh, I guess in substantial measure, I do," he replied. "The slovenliness of thinking on the Web. . . . When you destroy the basic philosophy, the parameters of a field of endeavor . . . everything changes. You stand on the cusp of a gigantic paradigm shift, where nothing is of the same value."

For copywriters like me, the Internet has been a boon: by allowing marketers to promote their products both on- and offline, it has created increased demand for copy, which is good for copywriters.

But I do think that several factors relating to the Internet have devalued what the market will pay for writing or other content, which is bad for writers, songwriters, and other content producers.

One factor is simply the fading-but-still-pervading culture of "everything should be free" on the Internet: if writing is given away for free, it's difficult to pay professionals a living wage to produce it.

The other Internet factor that works to reduce writers' fees is the temporary nature of online copy. If a company is hiring you to write their annual report, they are spending thousands of dollars on that document. And once it's printed, they have to live with it for a whole year. So the writing is very important, and they will pay you to get it right.

On the other hand, if you are writing a company description

for their Web site, they can post it at no charge. There is no printing cost. And they can change it at any time, also at no cost. Therefore, "getting it right" is less critical: if the writer doesn't deliver brilliance, they can always edit later.

Are blogs a powerful new tool for PR and branding online? Or is investing time and money in a business blog an utter waste?

It's certainly not an utter waste of time. But the reality is your resources for marketing, which basically boil down to time and money, are finite. Given that your financial and human resources are limited, you have to decide where to allocate them based on ROMD (return on marketing dollar).

My recommendation is that if blogging appeals to you, by all means start a blog as a secondary means of self-promotion. See whether you like doing it over the long term. If it's enjoyable and not a burden, then probably the blog will give you some benefit in excess of the time and money invested.

However, don't count on a blog to revolutionize your online marketing. The models for making money on the Internet have emerged and are beginning to be understood and embraced more widely. And so far, none of the proven models for making money online are built around a blog.

Rather, the successful e-commerce models I've seen typically involve some or all of the following elements: free content offers, a free e-newsletter, e-mail capture, search-engine optimization, pay-per-click advertising, e-zine advertising, landing pages, micro-sites, and Web sites. The blog is ancillary and strictly optional.

"If blogging is such a powerful medium, then it probably doesn't need a gaggle of bloggers blogging about how big a deal it is," writes David Murray in the *Ragan Report.* "The truth is, organizational blogging will move forward at its own pace and communicators don't need geeks whipping them in the behind while whipping themselves into a lather."[3]

What is the role of blogging in online marketing?

Blogs deliver two immediate benefits to an online marketing effort. The first is to position the blog author as an expert or guru in a specific topic or field.

You've heard it said about someone, "He wrote the book on the subject," implying that the person is an expert because he wrote the book. The basic method of establishing oneself as a guru is to selectively disseminate information on your topic through multiple media: books, articles, speeches, Web sites, and now blogs.

A blog alone is unlikely to make you the "go-to" guy or gal in your field. But neither is a speech, newsletter, book, or any other single publication. It's being frequently published in a wide range of venues that gradually builds awareness of you and establishes you as a guru in your field. A blog most likely can't do it alone. But today it certainly can help.

The second thing a blog can do for you is generate traffic to your Web site. If you have a Web site that is effective at converting traffic to leads or sales, the blog can then directly contribute to that revenue.

There's one other advantage of writing a blog worth mentioning: as a research tool.

If you blog, it gives you a chance to try out your ideas on a preliminary basis with an audience before you develop them into a longer, more permanent format, such as a content-rich

Web site, white paper, article, or book. A good portion of this book is material I first wrote on my blog as well as the comments of my blog readers in response to it.

Readers' comments are helpful not only to strengthen your writing but also for business planning and product development. If you discuss product features and application on your blog, your readers will tell you about features they'd like to see and applications they want to be able to handle with your product. A smart marketer listens to his customers, and a blog gives you a valuable place to hear them.

Will blogging ever match the effectiveness of online newsletters and e-mail marketing?

In my opinion, no.

The reason is simple: the model that works best for making money online today is to build a huge e-list of people who know you, and then market directly to them via either e-newsletters or e-mail marketing campaigns.

Internet-marketing entrepreneurs nationwide know the incredible value of the e-list; in most entrepreneurial online marketing businesses, your e-list is your most valuable asset.

According to Internet marketing expert Fred Gleeck, an e-list can generate between a dime and a dollar or more per name per month. Therefore, an e-list can be monetized, and the degree to which it can be monetized can be measured.

Blogs, on the other hand, do not enable you to capture the e-mail addresses and names of your readers. You do not own their names, nor do you have permission to send e-mail messages to them, as you do when someone opts into your list by subscribing to your e-newsletter.

Therefore, blogs cannot be monetized on a reliable and consistent basis. Yes, some bloggers make money with their blogs through a variety of means: building their credibility, PR, revenue from Google AdSense ads, banner ad sales, or being paid by a company to blog on their behalf.

By comparison, any Internet marketer, entrepreneurial or corporate, who understands and masters the e-mail marketing model, known alternatively as the "Agora Model" or "organic model," can make large sums of money on the Internet month after month, in a predictable, steady pattern. This is an advantage bloggers cannot as yet duplicate.

How much control do bloggers have over the blogosphere and the information flow within this global network?

Every blogger is free to link his blog to whatever other blogs he likes. That doesn't necessarily mean that those other bloggers are willing to reciprocate and link back to yours. So your control over the direction of the network is only in one direction—out from your blog extending to others.

My blog is set up so that anyone can post any comment he or she wishes without my permission or blessing: I don't preview the comments before they go up because I am too busy to do so, and frankly, it's not that important to me. Of course, if someone puts up a comment I don't want, I can delete it at my whim.

I know at least one marketing blogger who reads and approves all comments submitted to her blog before posting them. While this may seem to impede free speech, the Internet is not a total democracy. A blog requires space on a server and a domain name, and the person who is paying for those items, the blogger, should and does have the right to control them. The blog reader, who gets the blog free, does not.

That being said, my feeling is that prescreening blog comments is overkill: it overestimates the importance of what is published on your blog and probably overestimates the size of the audience reading your blog and the degree of attention they pay to it.

What is the effect of blogging and the Internet on writing as a profession and on publishing as an industry? Will people still pay for content when they can get all they want for free online?

It's a mixed bag. On the one hand, the Internet benefits content producers in general and writers in particular in several ways.

To begin with, blogging software (appendix F) makes it easy for anyone to publish, with virtually no financial investment or editorial approval by a traditional publisher. There are sites and blogs where you can pretty much post what you wish, and anyone with a hundred dollars can register a domain name and buy a year's worth of hosting for it.

On the other hand, as noted above, the Internet has in some ways reduced the economic value society places on writing and also diminished to some degree the market's willingness to pay for certain types of content. You can still sell content today and make good money doing it, but you have to work harder in your marketing to convince the market that your content is worth the asking price.

In the pre-Internet days, much of the content produced by writers was sold on the theme of "giving you (the reader) information you can't get elsewhere." The writer would do the legwork of spending hours in dusty libraries, researching information, and compiling it and condensing it into a clear, interesting, quick-reading article, paper, newsletter, or book. The reader didn't want to do this research himself and probably did not even know how.

Today, in the Internet age, information is easy to get: it's available all over the Web at no charge. So the writer's job is different, and the writer has to add value to content in different ways.

One way in which writers add value to content, and can therefore charge for it, is to save the reader time. The appeal is no longer "giving you information you can't get elsewhere"— because they can get it elsewhere—but that of saving time. Newsletter publishers, for instance, tell their potential subscribers: "We spend countless hours attending conferences, surfing the Internet, going to seminars, and reading dozens of periodicals and books, and then distill the information we obtain into a quick-reading monthly bulletin so you don't have to."

The other way to add value to content is through interpretation: you can sell your content if the reader perceives the author to be an authority or expert in the field. What the reader is paying for is not information per se, but knowledge, wisdom, and analysis.

If you want to be perceived as an expert at this level, writing a blog by itself won't do it. Reason: readers question the authority of blogs, believing that because anyone can launch and publish a blog, practically everyone is doing it. For a blogger to be seen as an authority, his blog must be accompanied by the other trappings of "guru-ship"—hosting a TV or radio show, having a content-rich Web site, being active on the lecture circuit, or writing magazine articles or books.

What is the future of blogging? Will it be a dominant marketing channel in a decade? Or will it soon go the way of the dodo and the dinosaur?

In an interview with *BtoB*, blogging consultant Deb Weil noted that there are two schools of thought concerning the future of blogging: "One is: blogs will revolutionize everything, changing the relationship between companies and customers. Another is: blogs are part of an incremental change in the way big companies talk to and interact with their companies and other constituencies."

Blogging consultants, thinkers, visionaries, and other pie-in-the-sky marketing types hold with the first school of thought: blogging is a business, communications, and marketing revolution. Too entrenched in their little blogging world, they fail to notice that blogs play little or no role in the majority of people's lives.

Practical, bottom-line, ROI-oriented marketers and businesspeople see blogging for what it really is: at best, an incremental improvement in a company's ability to reach and influence its market. Significant? Yes, especially considering the ease and low cost with which one can establish a company blog. Major? Hardly.

I think marketer Peter Delegge said it best: "Blog consultants are overhyping blogs beyond belief. Blogs are not a magic pill for marketing." Adds Graeme Thickins, CMO of GT&A Strategic Marketing: "Blogs may be one marketing tool of many, but they simply aren't going to replace all that came before."[4]

As the publicity Merriam-Webster gave blogging when it made the term its word of the year fades, and companies see the positive yet limited results blogging generates, the excitement surrounding blogging will also gradually fade.

I could not disagree more with Robert Scoble's assertion that "every company must have a blog." If you market online, a blog is purely optional—a frill rather than a focus of your online marketing campaign. To think otherwise is begging to be misled—and possibly in the process to shell out some big consulting fees for blogging advice and services you don't really need.

"This can be filed under the 'time will tell' category," says Bruce DeBoer, director of marketing at Synthesis Creative. "Some feel blogging is time they'll never get back, while others say it has raised their professional profile and connected them to some great clients.

"From my perspective, it's a method for adding a personal voice to an impersonal business and yet one more tool to widen the bandwidth of customer relations. At the very least, it's compelling, and that counts for something."

So blog if you want to. If you don't like blogs, don't bother. And if you think the advice in this book is great, and you want to let me know, or if you think I don't know beans about blogging and that my advice is useless, you can certainly say so— on my blog.

Best of luck to you in the blogosphere—and outside it!

NOTES

Introduction

1. "The Business of Blogging," *BusinessWeek*, 12/13/04.
1a. "Blog Tops Online Dictionary List," *Newsfactor Magazine*, 12/2/04.
2. Pew Internet & American Life Project, "Data Memo," 1/05.
3. Power, Tom, "Emerging Phenomenon: Search Engine Marketing Going Vertical," Illinois IT Association.
4. "Thomas Register to be Exclusively Online," *BtoB*, 5/31/05. http://netbob. comarticle.cms?articleId=24392
5. Joukhadar, Kristina, "Digital Tips for B-to-B," *Circulation Management*, 6/05, p. 20.
6. Epstein, Joseph, "Read This, It's Short," *The Wall Street Journal*, 6/23/04.
7. Comments made by David St. Lawrence to Bob Bly in personal correspondence and on St. Lawrence's blog.
8. G. B. Trudeau, *Doonesbury*, Universal Press Syndicate, © 2005.
9. Tad Clarke, editorial, *DM News*.
10. Personal conversation between Fred Gleeck and the author.

Chapter 1

1. *BuzzMachine*: results of ComScore study, reported 11/8/04.
2. Salerno, Frank, "What Could Go Wrong with Podcasting," *DM News*, 2/20/06, p. 16.
3. Garfinkel, David: private e-mail to Bob Bly, 12/2/04.
4. Jantsch, John: private e-mail to Bob Bly, 6/05/05.
5. Reader's Report, *Business Week*, 5/23/04, p. 24.
6. Magill, Ken, "Blogspeak Can Grave on the Blerves," *Direct*, 11/05, p. 20.
7. Gagnon, Eric, "Weblogs, Schmeblogs," *BMA Tuesday Marketing Notes*, 11/15/05.
8. Milne, James, "Weblogs and the Technology Cycle," University of South Florida dissertation, 3/04, pp. 42–49.

Chapter 2

1. Stone, B., *Blogging*. (Indianapolis: New Riders, 2002)
2. Hauptman, Don, "Opening a Can of Worms," *Word Ways*, 11/05.
3. Heine, Christopher, "Blogs Cut into Search Spending for Mindjet," *DM News*, 1/9/06, p. 14.
4. Usborne, Nick, "RSS Explained," *Excess Voice*, 3/16/05.
5. Khan, Mickey, "RSS Adoption Not Really That Simple," *DM News*, 3/21/05.

6. E-mail from Joel Heffner to Bob Bly, 1/12/05.
7. Weil, Deb, "Top 7 Tips to Write an Effective Blog," *BlogWrite for CEOs.*

Chapter 3

1. Cited in Chris Taylor, "10 Things We Learned About Blogs," *Time Magazine,* 12/19/04.
2. O'Malley, Gavin, "Marqui to Pay Bloggers for Mentioning Firm," *MediaDailyNews,* 21/1/04.
3. "Guinness Launches Weblog," *ad*RANTS, 2/17/06.
4. Blood, Rebecca, *The Weblog Handbook: Practical Advice on Creating and Maintaining Your Blog.* (New York: Perseus, 2001)
5. Macleod, Hugh, blog entry, www.gapingvoid.com (02/06)

Chapter 4

1. Oxfeld, Jesse, "Blah, Blah, Blog," *Editor & Publisher,* 4/7/05.
2. "Noted," *The Week,* 3/25/05, p. 18.

Chapter 5

1. Carr, David, "Need Some Luster? Try Rosie O'Donnell's Method," *The New York Times,* 3/10/05.

Chapter 6

1. Cargill, Bob, "The Case for Blogging," *Direct,* 6/05, pp. 45-46. Bob Cargill is a creative director, copywriter, and blogger from Sudbury, Massachusetts, and can be reached at Cargill123@aol.com. "Why Advertising, Marketing and PR Pros Should Blog" was published initially in December 2004 in Bob's blog, A Fine Kettle of Fish. His blog now goes by the name of A New Marketing Commentator and can be found on the Web at www.anewmarketingcommentator.com.
2. Rice, Jennifer: private e-mail to Bob Bly, 11/5/04.
3. Muldoon, Katie, "A Cataloger's Guide to Blogs and Wikis," *Direct,* 3/1/05, p. 36.
4. Sacks, Danielle, "Blogging Up," *Fast Company,* 5/05, p. 94.
5. Steere, Richard, "Marketing News to Advertisers," *NewsMax.com,* 2/22/06.

Chapter 7

1. Bob Lutz, "This Month in Optimize: Nothing to Fear from Executive Blogging" at: www.informationweek.com/story/showArticle.jhtml?articleID=165700961. (July, 2005).
2. www.blogwriteforces.com/blogwrite/fiels/yahoo-blog-guidelines.pdf
3. Pew Internet & American Life Project, November 2004

4. Backbone Media Survey by Turcotte, Cass & Munroe www.backbone-media.com

5. Needleman, Sarah, "Candidates Who Can Write in Conversational Style About Timely Topics Sought," *The Wall Street Journal*, June 6, 2005.

6. Ibid

7. *BusinessWeek* "Blogs Will Change Your Business" at: http://www.businessweek.com/magazine/content/05_18/b3931001_mz001.htm. (May 2005)

Chapter 8

1. Rall, Ted, "Bloggers and the New McCarthyism," *Yahoo! News*, 2/22/05.

Chapter 9

1. St. Lawrence, David: private e-mail to Bob Bly, 11/5/04.

2. Edwards, Jim, "The Dark Sides of Blogs," *The Net Reporter* E-zine, 10/11/05.

3. Weil, Debbie, "Beginner's Guide to Business Blogging," 2004–2005 WordBiz.com.

Chapter 10

1. Watlington, Amy, "A Rosy Future for RSS," *DM News Outlook* 2006, 2/13/06, pp. 28, 33. Reprinted with permission.

1a. Philipkoski, Kristen, "The Web Not the Death of Language," *Wired News*, 2/22/05.

2. Colanzi, John: private e-mail to Bob Bly, 10/06/04.

3. Murray, David: "Blog Wonks Need Chill Pill," *Ragan Report*, 12/6/04.

4. Delegge, Peter and Graeme Thickins: Letters to the Editor, *CMO Magazine*, 5/05, p. 6.

Glossary

1. Twist, Jo, "Looming Pitfalls of Work Blogs," BBC News, 1/3/05.

APPENDIX A

BOB BLY'S ANTIBLOGGING
COLUMNS FROM *DM NEWS*

First column, published 11/1/04
Can blogging help you market your product online?

Here's a question I've been curious about lately: should marketers add blogging to their arsenal of marketing tactics? Will it help sell more products and services?

Or is it—as I suspect—an utter waste of time? A pure vanity publication that won't pay you back even one thin dime for your effort?

First, a definition. "A blog is an online journal," explains blogging expert Deb Weil in her Business Blogging Starter Kit (www.wordbiz. com). "It's called a journal because every entry is time and date stamped and always presented in reverse chronological order."

The theory is that if you are an information marketer—or, if you publish information to establish your expertise in a niche industry or field—blogging should be part of your publishing arsenal.

According to Deb, a business blog is "a platform from which to lobby, network, and influence sales. It's a way to circumvent traditional media and analysts. And blogging can be done instantly, in real time, at a fraction of the cost of using traditional channels."

Now here's my hesitancy in recommending blogs as a marketing tool: I have yet to find a single marketer who says that a business blog has gotten him a positive ROI, or return on investment.

I know plenty of online marketers who make millions of dollars a year from their Web sites and e-zines, for instance. But I've not seen a blog whose creator says that the time and effort spent on their blog has directly put money into their pockets.

"I would say that, with few exceptions, blogs are not yet direct income producing resources in and of themselves," says blogging authority Paul Chaney (www.radiantmarketing.biz). "Their value lies in the fact that they help raise one's stature relative to their respective field."

In my observation, there are two major problems with blogging as a business-building tool.

The first is that most of the blogs I encounter are rambling, stream-of-consciousness musings about a particular topic of interest to the author, largely bereft of the kind of practical, pithy tips that e-zines, Web sites, and white papers offer.

As Deb says, reading the blog is like reading the author's journal or diary. And unless you are a guru or celebrity whom others worship from afar, people are simply not going to flock to your blog to discover your latest thoughts on life.

The second problem with blogs is one of distribution.

With an e-zine, once the reader subscribes, he gets the e-zine delivered to him electronically every week or every month—or however often you send it.

But with a blog, the reader has to go out and proactively look for it. And since your contributions to your blog may be irregular and unscheduled, he has no way of knowing when something new of interest has been added. [author's note: At this point I did not know about RSS feeds. Once bloggers pointed out the error, I maintained that RSS feeds at the time were too complex for many non-techie users, under-publicized, and not known to the majority of Internet users.]

One big advantage of blogs, according to Paul Chaney, is that having a blog can help pull traffic to your Web site.

"The search engines, especially Google, love blogs," says Paul. "You'd be amazed at how many of your posts will end up in the top ten returns. If search engine optimization is a concern to you, blogs are the best way I know to move up the ladder as well as increase your page rank."

"I confidently predict that blogs will soon be a key piece of an effective online marketing strategy," says Deb Weil. "Ultimately, they're nothing more than an instant publishing tool, one that makes posting fresh content to the Web within anyone's reach. No tech skill or knowledge required."

And that's another one of my complaints with blogs in particular and the Web in general: the ease with which people can post and disseminate content. "The best thing about the Web is that anyone can publish on it; the worst thing about the Web is that anyone can publish on it," a computer magazine columnist once observed.

The problem is that there is already too much content, and we don't want or need more. Analysis, wisdom, insight, advice, strategies, ideas—yes. But raw information, data, or content—no. And from what I can see, blogs serve up almost none of the former, and tons of the latter.

Blogs are, by virtue of being a form of online diary, like diaries: rambling, incoherent, and more suited for private thoughts than public consumption.

If you have something of value to share, there are many better formats for doing it online than by blogging, including white papers, e-zines, and Web sites.

Even bulletin boards are interactive, so they have value by virtue of shared opinions, dialogue, and engaging conversation that may be listened to openly and publicly.

But most blogs seem to be the private idiosyncratic musings of an individual, without censure or editing of any kind. And the result is like porridge: a gloppy mess, tasteless, and not very satisfying.

Until that changes, I can't see starting and maintaining a blog of your own, unless you are bored and looking for something to do, or require an outlet for self-expression. And if the latter is the case, well . . . why not just buy and keep a diary instead?

Second column, published 12/6/04

Blogging redux

In a recent *DM News* column, I apparently offended a segment of the blogging community by suggesting that perhaps blogs might be "an utter waste of time . . . a pure vanity publication that won't pay you back even one thin dime for your effort."

Here's what all the hoopla has taught me so far: bloggers are a tight-knit community that sticks together and are rabidly enthusiastic about their medium. Many are self-described blogging "evangelists."

Their attitude toward new and untested marketing media and channels is probably a lot different than yours and mine (I assume that you, like me, are a direct marketer).

I told virtually every blogger who said I had treated blogging unfairly the following. . . .

"We direct marketers only care about one thing in marketing: ROI (return on investment).

"Unless a dollar spent on a marketing test returns two or three dollars in revenues, we consider that test a failure—and cut off the promotion."

For instance, there are direct marketers generating millions of dollars a year in direct product sales from e-zines and e-mail marketing campaigns. One I know produces upwards of $40 million in annual sales from their e-mail marketing.

I challenged the bloggers: "Can anyone out there show me even a single blog that produces one percent of that—$400,000 annual sales?"

No takers, so far. Not a single blogger could produce evidence of a blog generating a significant, positive ROI (the cut-off figure for which I have chosen direct sales of $400,000 a year or more).

But what my challenge *did* produce was a bunch of passionate responses explaining to me why blogging is without question the next big thing in marketing despite its lack of discernible ROI.

"It's all about the conversation," writes Marc Orchant, feeding me *The Cluetrain Manifesto*'s party line. "That's the point of the blog space. As a lifelong marketer myself, I find the DM industry behind the curve, generally speaking, when it comes to embracing disruptive technologies." Reader B. L. Ochman says, "Blogs help develop a conversation between a company and its customers [and] have become an important part of the marketing mix."

As direct marketers, I'm not sure our primary objective is to embrace disruptive technologies or have conversations. Isn't it more about boosting response, generating a positive ROI, and beating the control?

"My argument is that blogging is more likely to raise brand awareness, but that the impact on direct sales will be more difficult to assess," says Max Blumberg. "Therefore, I don't think it is appropriate to look for a close relationship between blogging and direct sales."

Some of the writers who contacted me were eager to compare blogging to direct mail and show me that DM is inferior. Blogger Yvonne DiVita states, "The small business owner cannot hope to create and support a continuing successful direct mail campaign."

I'd recommend Yvonne start reading *DM News*; every issue is packed with stories of businesses large and small making healthy profits with both traditional direct mail as well as e-mail marketing.

Yvonne also told me that when she was a corporate assistant to the CEO of a good-sized company, "I threw all the direct mail in the circular file at my feet. The CEO didn't want to see it. So, who's really reading your client's direct mail piece?"

Yvonne seems unaware of the concepts of cost per thousand and break-even analysis, which let us direct marketers make a healthy profit even if 98 out of 100 prospects toss our mailings away without a second glance. She comments, "When a direct mail piece can only assure the sender of approximately a 2% to 3% return, you can't convince me the hundreds or thousands spent on it is worth it." Tell that to Omaha Steaks, Covenant House, and Philips!

Jennifer Rice explains that comparing blogs with direct marketing is to look at blogs from the wrong angle: "Blogging is not a direct response vehicle. It's an awareness, visibility, and promotion vehicle that happens to be terrific for those of us selling intellectual capital. It's also extremely useful for corporations to use as a means to connect with customers and get feedback."

Finally, a couple of resources to help you learn more about blogs (I recommend both highly).

First, Deb Weil's "Business Blogging Starter Kit," available at www.wordbiz.com. Deb is a blogging evangelist, but her kit contains a lot of useful how-to guidance for anyone thinking about starting a blog.

Second, get B. L. Ochman's special report, "What Could Your Company Do with a Blog?" Like Deb's, detailed, specific, and instructional. Available at www.whatsnextonline.com.

Recently Ms. Ochman asked me, "Do you still think blogs are baloney?" I replied: "I never thought or actually said they were baloney. I just said that, as a direct marketer, I don't think blogging—a medium with unproven ROI and uneven quality—is something we should get excited about, as the blogosphere has.

"I think members of the blogosphere should be applauded for their pioneering spirit . . . but their evangelical enthusiasm is not yet supported by results."

I'm still highly skeptical about the whole blogging thing, and I find the majority of blogs to be lacking in quality and content (to be fair, there are many exceptions here). But I do think the topic warrants further investigation on my part, which includes starting my own blog at www.bly.com/blog/blog.htm. I'll keep you posted and report periodically in this column—and of course, on my blog.

APPENDIX B

RULES OF THE BLOGOSPHERE

1. Not everyone blogs or reads blogs, but often bloggers operate as if their blogs are reaching everyone.
2. Many bloggers believe that the Internet is better than print, period.
3. Add a new post to your blog once or twice a week. Never go more than ten days without adding a new post.
4. A blog is not going to reach all your customers. The only way to ensure you reach every customer is through direct marketing, e.g., sending an e-mail, postcard, or letter to your house file (customer mailing list).
5. Blogging, like public relations and image advertising, may have a substantial effect on your business, but the precise ROI is extremely difficult to measure.
6. Blogs are, by nature, contentious. Arguments, opinions, and strongly held points of view all play well to the blog audience.
7. A significant segment of the blogosphere considers itself exempt from the normal rules of conversational etiquette and polite behavior as practiced in all other forms of communication including conversation and e-mail.
7a. Copyright laws apply everywhere, offline and online, including the blogosphere: just because you aren't selling your blog content doesn't mean you can post copyrighted material belonging to others without their permission.
8. Bloggers consider conversation, not selling, to be the most effective form of marketing products and services online.
8a. To be effective marketing vehicles, blogs should be free of marketing. They should contain useful content and the truth,

not hype or sales talk. To violate this rule not only costs you sales and credibility, but it also incurs the disdain and wrath of the blogosphere.

9. If your goal in blogging is not mere self-expression but to influence others, the type of blog you should write (in order of influence) should be political, technology, or business.

10. The key to getting results from a business blog is to define the results you want to get before you start. Do you want to increase online sales by generating more traffic on your Web site? Create a favorable image for your company or product? Get your side of the story out in an honest manner to combat bad PR? Keep your employees, vendors, customers, investors, and other stakeholders up to date on company activities and plans?

11. Don't believe those who tell you, "Every business needs a blog." The truth is, you *don't* need a blog—and you'll do fine without one.

12. For blogs centering on a specific topic or subject, the ideal author is a subject-matter expert (SME) who can write, rather than a writer who has to rely on subject-matter experts for content. Reason: the SME's more intimate knowledge allows him to comment spontaneously on the subject as the spirit moves him, which is how good blogs are written.

13. Grammar, spelling, punctuation, and the other rules of written communication apply to blogs just as they do everywhere else. The reader who spots typos and misspellings will not think you are casual or relaxed about matters of grammar and proofreading; he will think you are a sloppy and careless writer—and by extension, a sloppy, careless thinker—not the impression you want to convey.

14. Blogging is just one more method of communicating online. And it is one of the minor methods, not—like Web sites, e-newsletters, and e-mail marketing—one of the "killer apps" of Internet marketing.

APPENDIX C

BLOGGING GUIDES,
BOOKS, E-BOOKS, AND
HOW-TO REPORTS

How to Master RSS (FifteenDegrees-North, 2003, 59 pages, Fifteen Degrees North Professional Web Design Company (www.15dn.cm). Shows you how to use RSS, create your RSS feed, and submit your blog to get listed on RSS directories.

Rebecca Blood and the editors of Perseus Publishing, *We've Got Blog* (Perseus Publishing, 2002, 242 pages, $20). Collection of essays from various authors on the blogging phenomenon.

Harry Baisden, *NEPA's Guide to E-Zines, E-Newsletters, and B-Blogs,* (Newsletter & Electronic Publishers Association, 2004, 49 pages, www.newsletters.org). Collection of articles on how to use blogs and e-zines to sell high-priced information products online.

Rebecca Blood, *The Weblog Handbook* (Perseus Books Group, 2002, 144 pages, $14). A thoughtful analysis of blogging by an early blogging evangelist; includes tips and advice for the blogging newbie.

Meryl K. Evans, *How to Start a Business Blog and Build Traffic* (Meryl.net, 2004, 16 pages). Particularly valuable are the sections on how to launch and publicize a brand-new blog.

Matthew Haughey, Paul Bausch, Meg Hourihan, *We Blog: Publishing Online with Weblogs* (John Wiley & Sons, 2002, 350 pages, $20). A how-to blogging guide with favorable reviews on Amazon.

Hugh Hewitt, *Blog: Understanding the Information Reformation That's Changing Your World* (Nelson Books, 2005, 225 pages). Sociological commentary on blogs as a tool for change in communications, journalism, politics, and the media.

Biz Stone, *Blogging: Genius Strategies for Instant Web Content* (Pearson

Education, 2002, 336 pages, $29.99). One of the first how-to books for blogging enthusiasts.

Weil, Deb, *Beginner's Guide to Business Blogging* (WordBiz, 2005, 38 pages, $29, www.wordbiz.com). A concise guide on how to start and write a successful business blog.

Business Blogging Starter Kit (WordBiz, 2005, 128 pages, $147, www.wordbiz.com). An expanded, more in-depth version of the manual above.

ROI of Business Blogging (WordBiz, 2005, 131 pages, $197, www.wordbiz.com). Similar to the above manual, but with increased focus on how to generate ROI from a business blog.

APPENDIX D

BLOGGING CONSULTANTS WHO CAN HELP YOU SET UP AND WRITE YOUR BLOG

Click Here
8750 N. Central Expressway
Suite 1200
Dallas, TX 75231
E-mail: info@clickhere.com
Tel: 214-891-7625
Fax: 214-891-5333
Web: www.clickhere.com

Derek Scruggs
Escalan, LLC
959 W. Moorhead Circle
Suite D
Boulder, CO 80305
Tel: 303-543-1186
Cell: 303-808-6614
E-Mail: derek@escalan.com

Tom Kane, President
Kane Consulting, Inc.
P.O. Box 50834
Sarasota, FL 34232
Tel: 941-376-3366
E-mail:
tkane@KaneConsultingInc.com
Web: http://www.legalmarketing
blog.com/

Tris Hussey
Managing Director
Qumana Services
330-1639 West 2nd Ave.
Vancouver, BC V6J 1H3
Tel: 250-537-1234
E-mail: tris@qumana.com
Web: http://blog.qumana.com
Skype: tris.hussey

Bruce DeBoer
Director of Marketing and Business
   Development
Synthesis
112 South Blount Street
Suite 101
Raleigh, NC 27601
E-mail:
bruce@synthesiscreative.com
Cell: 919-523-6385
Tel/Office: 919-832-8533
Fax: 919-829-8299
Web:
http://www.synthesiscreative.com
   /index.php

Tony Dowler Consulting
2716 E. Union St.
Seattle, WA 98122
E-mail: tony.dowler@gmail.com
Web: http://tonydowler.
   blogspot.com/

APPENDIX E

BUSINESS BLOGS EVERY BLOGGING
NEWBIE SHOULD READ

*ad*RANTS
http://www.adrants.com/index.php?show_id=107849860946826702

B. L. OCHMAN'S WEBLOG
http://www.whatsnextblog.com/

B2B LEAD GENERATION BLOG
http://blog.startwithalead.com

BLOGADS WEBLOG
http://Weblog.blogads.com/Weblog.php

BLOGS4BIZ
http://www.blogs4biz.blogspot.com/

BLOGWRITE FOR CEOS
http://blogwrite.blogs.com/

CORANTE
http://www.corante.com/strange/archives/cat_blogging.php

DANA'S BLOG
http://www.danavan.net/Weblog/archives/cat_blogging.html

DEBBIE WEIL'S BLOG
http://www.debbieweil.com/

DIVA MARKETING
http://www.bloombergmarketing.blogs.com/

DUCT TAPE MARKETING
http://www.ducttapemarketing.com/Weblog.php

HARRY JOINER
http://www.marketingheadhunter.com/

J. S. LOGAN
http://www.jslogan.com/

LIP-STICKING
http://www.windsormedia.blogs.com/lipsticking/2004/04/new_book_on
_blo.html

MAX BLUMBERG'S BLOG
http://maxblumberg.typepad.com/dailymusings/2004/11/an_interchange
_.html

MICRO PERSUASION
http://www.micropersuasion.com/

MKTG BRAINLOG
http://www.mktg.idared.net/archives/cat_everything_else.html

NEVILLE HOBSON'S BLOG
http://www.nevillehobson.com

RADIANT MARKETING BLOG
http://radiantmarketing.typepad.com/radiant_marketing/2004/11/bob_bly
_blogs.html

RIPPLES
http://ripples.typepad.com/ripples/2004/01/blogging_their_.html

SMALL BUSINESS BRANDING
http://smallbusinessbranding.typepad.com/

SUSAN GETGOOD'S BLOG
http://getgood.typepad.com/getgood_strategic_marketi/

THE DIARY OF A SLIGHTLY OFF CENTRE INTERNET MARKETER...
http://www.15dn.com/15dnBlog/

THE MANEUVER MARKETING COMMUNIQUÉ
http://twoscenarios.typepad.com/maneuver_marketing_commun/

THE POWERLOG DAHBLOG
http://powerwriting.com/gm/

TSMI'S TRADE SHOW MARKETING REPORT
http://tsmi.blogs.com/

SOME NOTEWORTHY CORPORATE BLOGS TO CHECK OUT

BOEING
http://www.boeing.com/randy/

GENERAL MOTORS
http://fastlane.gmblogs.com/

SUN MICROSYSTEMS
http://blogs.sun.com/jonathan

BLOG SEARCH ENGINES AND SUBSCRIPTION SITES

FEEDSTER
www.feedster.com

GOOGLE
www.blogsearch.google.com

ICE ROCKET
www.icerocket.com

OPEN MIND
www.openmind.com

PUBSUB
www.pubsub.com

TECHNORATI
www.technorati.com

APPENDIX F

BLOGGING PLATFORMS AND SOFTWARE

Blogger
http://www.blogger.com/start

Blogware
http://home.blogware.com/

FactoSystem Weblog
http://sourceforge.net/projects/factor

GeekLog
http://sourceforge.net/projects/geeklog

InstaBlog
http://instablog.hit.bg/

OpenJournal
www.grohol.com/downloads/oj/

TypePad
www.typepad.com

WordPress
http://wordpress.org/

APPENDIX G

GLOSSARY OF BLOGGING TERMS

archives. Sidebar link to previous posts, organized by day, week, or month

blog. Web site assembled from short, frequent posts; characterized by reader comments, numerous links, and RSS syndication

categories. Sidebar links to previous posts displayed by topic

comments. Ability of readers to agree or disagree with specific posts. Comments can instantly appear or must first be approved.

description. Text identifying blog content or purpose, with keywords to attract search engines

display name. Blogs and comments posted under a screen name instead of an actual name

dooce. To be "dooced" means to have lost your job for something you wrote on your blog[1]

draft. Posts are usually immediately published, but you can save unfinished posts for publishing later, after completion.

forms. You create posts by entering titles and text into online text boxes that are automatically formatted when published.

keywords. Terms appropriate to your market, included in titles, descriptions, and posts to attract search-engine traffic

links. Text accessing Web site pages, downloadable files, e-mail links, or other posts in your own—or another's—blog

news aggregator. Software that permits subscribers to scan a single file containing posts and comments from several blogs

news readers. Software that permit subscribers to scan the headlines, and—often—initial sentences of recent posts

permalink. Web addresses of individual posts, so others can refer to specific posts in their blogs See Trackback

ping. Software feature that automatically notifies search engines when new posts or comments have been published

podcasting. Emerging RSS technology that syndicates MP-3 audio files

post. Posts are the building blocks of blogs. Each post is a separate Web page with a specific URL See Permalink

quickpost. Feature that makes it easy to link specific Web pages to posts created while surfing

romd. Return on marketing dollars: the amount of sales or profits generated by a promotion versus the cost of that promotion

rss. Real Simple Syndication; popular format for announcing blog updates to others

sidebar. Information like e-mail and background links, archives, and categories, placed to the left, right, or both sides of posts

status. After creating a post, you can immediately publish it, save it as an unpublished draft, or publish it at a specific time on a specific future date

syndicate. RSS feature that automatically informs subscribers when new posts or comments have been published on your blog

team blog. Blogs written and published by more than one author, such as members of a research team or sales force

template. Feature that provides consistent formatting and structure for posts, defining colors, content, layout, and typography

timestamp. Time and date information automatically added to posts and comments

trackback. Feature, based on Permalinks, that lets you keep track of references to your posts in the blogs of others

typelist. Sidebar links to recommended resources like recommended books, glossaries, URLs, photographs, or individuals

About the Author

ROBERT W. BLY has more than twenty-five years experience as a copywriter specializing in direct marketing. His clients include IBM, Lucent Technologies, Nortel Networks, SurfControl, Medical Economics, BOC Gases, Praxair, Casey Research, Agora, Weiss Research, Passlogix, and Sony.

He has won numerous marketing awards, including the Standard of Excellence Award from the Web Marketing Association and an IMMY from the Information Marketing Association. Bob is the author of more than sixty books, including *The Complete Idiot's Guide to Direct Marketing* (Alpha) and *The Online Copywriter's Handbook* (McGraw-Hill).

Bob Bly publishes a monthly online newsletter, *The Direct Response Letter*, with more than forty thousand subscribers. He is a regular columnist for *Early to Rise* and *DM News*. His articles have appeared in *Amtrak Express*, *Cosmopolitan*, *Computer Decisions*, *Writer's Digest*, and many other publications.

A frequent speaker, Bob has presented to such organizations as the Direct Marketing Club of New York, Publicity Club of New York, Direct Marketing Association, and the U.S.

Army. He is a member of the American Institute of Chemical Engineers, Business Marketing Association, and Newsletter and Electronic Publishers Association.

Before becoming an independent copywriter, Mr. Bly was a marketing communications representative at Westinghouse and an advertising manager at Koch Engineering. He has also taught copywriting at New York University.

Questions and comments about *Blog, Schmog!* may be sent to:

Bob Bly
Copywriter
22 E. Quackenbush Avenue
Dumont, NJ 07628
Phone: 201-385-1220
Fax: 201-385-1138
E-mail: rwbly@bly.com
Web site: www.bly.com
Blog: www.bly.com/blog/blog.htm

Acknowledgments

As always, thanks to my agent, Bob Diforio, for playing matchmaker between the publisher and me.

Thanks also to my editors, Brian Hampton, Paula Major, and Bryan Norman, for making this book much better than it was when the manuscript first crossed their desks—and for their patience in waiting for it to get there.

Special thanks to Paul Wodehouse, Derek Scruggs, Susan Getgood, Bruce DeBoer, Bob McCarthy, Harry Joiner, Tom Kane, Steve Slaunwhite, and the other readers of my blog—especially those whose posts on Bob Bly's Blog I quote throughout this book. Most of the marketing experts and others whose blogging opinions are quoted in this book first expressed those opinions my blog, unless otherwise noted.